# Why Alaska?

## *Life on the Last Frontier*

A Collaboration by
C. David Gleason and
DeAnn M. Gleason

**Fish Creek
Publishing**
WASILLA, ALASKA

Although the author and publisher have made every effort to ensure the accuracy and completeness of information contained in this book, we assume no responsibility for errors, inaccuracies, omissions, or any inconsistency herein. Any slighting of people, places, or organizations is unintentional.

First printing 2005


ISBN 0-9709438-8-1
LCCN 2005926396

**ATTENTION CORPORATIONS, UNIVERSITIES, COLLEGES, AND PROFESSIONAL ORGANIZATIONS:** Quantity discounts are available on bulk purchases of this book for educational, gift purposes, or as premiums for increasing magazine subscriptions or renewals. Special books or book excerpts can also be created to fit specific needs. For information, please contact Fish Creek Publishing, P.O. Box 871007, Wasilla, AK 99687; 907-376-3071.

# DEDICATION

To Marie Drake, author of *Alaska's Flag,*
the official song of the State of Alaska:

*Eight stars of gold on a field of blue…*
*Alaska's flag. May it mean to you*
*The blue of the sea, the evening sky,*
*The mountain lakes, and the flow'rs nearby;*
*The gold of the early sourdough's dreams,*
*The precious gold of the hills and streams;*
*The brilliant stars in the northern sky,*
*The "Bear"…the "Dipper"…and, shining high,*
*The great North Star with its steady light,*
*Over land and sea a beacon bright,*
*Alaska's flag…to Alaskans dear,*
*The simple flag of a last frontier.*

# ACKNOWLEDGMENTS

Having been blessed with numerous personal and professional friends who helped open many doors, leaves us with a much longer list of people we need to thank than space permits.

First, we would like to thank our parents and grandparents for encouraging us to be all we could be. The self-confidence they helped instill has enabled us to succeed beyond our wildest dreams.

Walter Witt, who spent so many hours tutoring DeAnn, deserves much credit for her success.

Donald Jarvis, Bill Carroll, Del Burch, Charlie Carpenter, Ozzie Osborne, and Chuck Schuman, all dedicated sponsors of C. David's rise to stardom in the communications industry, cannot be thanked enough.

Special thanks to Kurt Wagner for the black-and-white cover drawing of the old Jensen cabin in Talkeetna.

Finally, without the continuing encouragement of our dear friend Pat Coy, the writing of this book, and C. David's earlier book *Why Russia?: A Nostalgic Old World Adventure,* would not have been possible.

# TABLE OF CONTENTS

# PREFACE

For thirty-three years, C. David dreamed of living in Alaska, the "last frontier." For the past thirty-five years he and DeAnn have lived that dream. Overcoming the hardships of the first few years, together they managed to build a wonderful life for their children and themselves.

Though fraught with many setbacks, life in Alaska has been, overall, a very rewarding journey. Their story, though unique, is not much different from one most of their close friends can identify with.

It is their hope others will enjoy reading about the life they have enjoyed living.

CHAPTER 1

# Rearranging Priorities

*It was the morning* of July 17, 1993, our thirty-eighth wedding anniversary. When I, C. David, awoke in my dark little Russian flat, a whole new phase of my life was born. Having nothing else to do but wait for confirmation on the Alaska Airlines flight out of that hellhole, I was left with plenty of free time to reflect on my past, present, and future life. Self-recriminations by a man who had spent a large part of his life shooting himself in the foot were at the top of my list.

My thoughts drifted back to my childhood, which could well have been the basis for the TV series *The Waltons.* I am convinced the writers stole the whole idea from my family, sort of. One reason for the popularity of *The Waltons* was that many of my generation grew up under those same wonderful family circumstances. I only watched the program a few times. I couldn't handle it. Grown men are not supposed to cry.

Much of my nostalgia is rooted in the fact that I really was raised on a small Midwestern farm. My father and grandfather had adjacent farms. They had a sawmill that provided the financing required to run the rest of the farms. Together with my two brothers, James and Michael, I was forced to work hard on those farms. My father repeatedly stated, "I am raising you guys to be tough as nails, and you'll thank me for it someday." Many times during my life this has proven to be a true statement.

Most Sundays were centered around attending church and returning home to eat chicken and dumplings at my paternal grandmother's table. As I sat in my flat on that July morning, I could almost smell those Sunday dinners mixed with the ever-present, musty leather-like "smell of Russia" that permeated everything in the flat. This smell always followed me home to become a constant reminder of Russia whenever I opened one of my suitcases.

This musty leather-like smell invariably brought my thoughts back to a childhood where my father and grandfather were rather well known "horse traders," which allowed my brothers and me to always have horses to ride. We would pretend to be Roy Rogers, Gene Autry, or Hopalong Cassidy on real horses, not the "broom-stick horses" most of our childhood friends made-do with.

The most exciting times I remember about those halcyon child-hood years were the hunting and fishing trips we took with my father and his buddies. I always felt closer to my father at these times. Being a part of the comradeship between old friends who had grown up together was something I was to lose by moving away from my hometown at an early age. In Siberia I had managed to regain some of this lost male companionship.

My childhood holidays were always some huge affair with my father's entire family. All the aunts and uncles, cousins, my parents, and my brothers and I would truck to "Ma and Pa," as everyone referred to my father's parents. There was always a huge fresh-cut Christmas tree with hundreds of presents underneath. The long old oak table was piled high with turkey, gravy, dumplings, biscuits, gelatin, cranberry sauce, sweet potatoes, homemade pickles and other foods too numerous to mention.

I cannot recall an unpleasant thing about those family holidays. So why was it I preferred to be at my maternal grandmother Wolcott's side? She always had a little fake white Christmas tree with blue lights sitting on top of her giant Philco radio. The meal was, "Let's see what's in the refrigerator."

You would always find one very neatly wrapped present under the small tree with your name on it. She would somehow make it appear that you were the only grandchild she had bought a gift for. It must have been quite a logistics problem for her to arrange this, since I am certain she played the same "special attentions" game with each of her eleven grandchildren. The present was always a book or some similar gift to encourage you to use your mind. All time spent with her was also, I suppose, a little welcome relief from the "raised tough" farm life. She never tired of spending hour upon hour filling my mind with stories involving high morality and lofty ambitious themes. She had many favorite bromides, such as "You are what you think you are." This was very heavy stuff, which if believed, tends to give one a certain feeling of indestructibility when dealing with most of life's little problems. It works even better than the "tough guy" thing or, at least, compliments it. The combination of these teachings by my maternal grandmother and my father must have taken firm rooting, because whatever I have wished, worked, and prayed for hard enough...I have gotten.

It did not always turn out to be what I wanted, however. One great example being my presently lying in wait, in a dingy room, anticipating a flight back to the real world.

It was time to change direction in life...again.

CHAPTER 2

# Love & Marriage:
## *Father Really Does Know Best*

*More waiting for the* Alaska Airlines flight brought more memories.

In high school, during the fabulous fifties, I was considered to be three things: a Romeo, an honor student, and a questionable athlete. I used the questionable athlete's status to date nearly every cheerleader in the county…at least once. Impulsive and reckless!

All impulsive and reckless people must have a confidant. Take my word for it. My friend and confidant, DeAnn, was another borderline genius like me. Being a natural born leader, she was an officer in every organization she belonged to, which left no time to "waste" as a cheerleader. She was also one of those rare young girls so beautiful even she didn't believe it. This lovely redhead possessed a keen mind in a petite, smooth, creamy skinned and beautiful body. Her soft green eyes somehow saw in me what my grandmother predicted I could be. She was the first person with whom I ever felt at ease discussing my own deep and abiding faith in God, because her own faith and acceptance of God's will were so open and natural. This never-wavering faith of hers has, through the years, helped to maintain and strengthen my own. It has also undoubtedly given her the stamina required to follow me all over the world.

Much as I'd like to take all the credit for asking my DeAnn to become my wife…sometimes, impulsive and reckless-abandon people do listen to parents and grandparents. My confidant and I had the leads in our senior high school play. After watching the play, my father asked me why I had never dated *her*. "She would never date me," I scoffed.

"You are missing the best one, Davie. If you do not grab her up someone else will and you'll regret that for the rest of your life. If you marry her, I will make you a full partner in my new construction company," Dad promised.

My father had recently begun to turn the smallest of his farms into building lots and construct new homes on them. His favorite saying had now become, "The only thing ever raised that made money on these farms is building lots."

Following Dad's advice and constant urging, I began to cautiously move toward suggesting DeAnn and I might try dating. For the first time in my life the ever-confident ladies' man reputation I had honed and cultivated failed. My first stumbling attempt to ask DeAnn for a date was a disaster. She misunderstood my intent, thinking I was trying to ask her to help me get a date with one of her friends! For several days she avoided me. With her mother's help I was finally able to convince her I was asking *her* to our senior prom. From there on everything was uphill. Friendship blossomed into love.

Marriage had not really been a part of my plans, but then I actually had no "plan" other than feeling I should take advantage of my scholarship and attend Allegheny State Teachers College to become a teacher of math or science. I decided to make a deal with my father. "If I do marry DeAnn and go into business with you, will you pay for my college education?" He agreed. So what was my next step? I supposed it might be a good idea to let the love of my life know about the plans we were making for her. She might not agree.

First, I needed to take DeAnn to meet my Grandma Wolcott, as I had done with several girls over the years. Nearly every time, all I had received from her was a meaningful roll of her eyes indicating disapproval. I wasn't certain what to expect this time, but was pleasantly surprised at her reaction. She fell more in love—if possible—than I had. Probably the most impulsive and reckless-abandon thing I have ever done was to ask my lovely DeAnn to marry me while we were still in high school. To my surprise she replied, "Yes."

On July 17, 1955, one month after graduating from high school, the beautiful young girl married me. I cherished everything about this lovely creature with green eyes and milky white skin. She wore her auburn hair and Irish temperament, inherited from her father, with a graceful dignity obtained through an unshakable faith in God and a firm belief that all human beings will eventually do the right thing if given a chance. The latter she inherited from her Ukrainian mother.

Both of our fledgling careers, which had been years in the planning—mine as a teacher and hers as a nurse—took a sharp and permanent detour.

# CHAPTER 3

# Our Early Years

*For two years my* father's construction company did quite well. I worked on all phases of home building as a carpenter, mason, sheet rock installer, electrician, and plumber. Dad did pay for me to attend a nearby technical college evenings and by correspondence to obtain an associate degree in electrical engineering.

By mid 1957 the building boom in our area was grinding to a standstill. My father took a job with the city and cast me adrift. By chance, I had become acquainted with a telephone lineman named Bill in whose section we were building a home very close to a buried cable. The fellow was constantly stopping by to make certain we would not cut his cable while digging to install foundations, septic systems, and well lines. He took a liking to me and we spent several hours discussing my future plans (of which I really had none, other than to complete this final home). He eventually suggested that, with my electrical background, I might want to apply for a local position opening with AT&T. I was somewhat ashamed to admit I had no idea what AT&T was.

Bill made arrangements for me to take a Greyhound bus to downtown Cleveland and a cab to 750 Huron Street for an interview. My young knees were knocking as I approached the

Our first home, Ohio Lake Erie—1957.

thirty-story building with the polished brass plaque proudly displaying "American Telephone and Telegraph," inscribed beneath the engraved bell. I took the elevator to the eleventh floor (where I would one day in the near future be the supervisor) and met with my interviewer. I was exposed to the Wonderlic testing system for the first time. Wonderlic was designed to test your IQ. Mine tested at 150, which I later learned was considered borderline genius. Several electrical and electronic tests followed. After the testing, the interviewer informed me I was to be hired at an entry-level position in the Geneva AT&T office, if I was interested. This position paid only $49.50 per week but included a free hospitalization plan and a free retirement plan. Also, all long distance phone calls would be paid for by the company. Best of all, Geneva was our hometown. To DeAnn and me this all seemed too good to be true.

To further enhance our good luck, after meeting DeAnn, my new boss hired her as the office secretary. A few months later a good friend of mine, Jack Lingle, was hired to fill a second opening at the office. His wife, Margie, was a wonderful person who immediately formed what has become a lifelong friendship with DeAnn. Over the next three years our second son Lee and daughter Jeannie were born. The Lingles were blessed with a daughter the same age as our Jeannie. The four of us did everything together. Work became a pleasant experience, as did our social and family life.

We hired three more technicians over the next two years. As lead tech, everyone reported to me in the supervisor's absence. At that time, I was an easy boss who gladly shared equally in the duties with everyone else.

Because of my high test scores, my obvious ability to grasp the newly emerging microwave telecommunications technology, my natural gift for teaching others, and the good luck to work for unselfish bosses, I began to develop a high profile in the company. I was asked to teach company schools, write technical papers, and attend strategic planning seminars. For a little old farm boy of twenty-one or -two this was very heady stuff. At one of the seminars I must have impressed someone of importance and power in the company. At age twenty-three, I was offered a first-level management position in Sandusky, the largest maintenance district in

Ohio. This would require moving to the opposite side of the state. There were probably ten reasons not to take this promotion, for every reason in favor.

Both sets of grandparents adored our children. To my parents, who had never traveled very far outside the county, the thought of our leaving our hometown was nearly devastating. The promotion would increase our income very little as DeAnn would become unemployed. If she did go back to work in our new location, we would incur babysitting costs because we were moving away from free grandma and younger-sister babysitters. The list of disadvantages went on and on. Naturally, I took the job. Impulsive and reckless? Possibly.

Being kind to myself, I will merely say as a full-time supervisor at age twenty-three, I was *not* an easy boss to work for. As a technician and as a new supervisor, I lived for my job. I always worked long hours on my own, many without pay. I was extremely demanding of myself. It was only natural I would expect the same from all those reporting to me.

Unfortunately, this is not a perfect world and very few people in it are as dedicated as I was. By pushing myself and my people to the limit of their endurance, and making many enemies, our maintenance district received several awards over the next three years. My superiors could not have been more pleased. The company rewarded me by making me one of the highest paid first-level supervisors in the central area. When AT&T decided to start a Management Assessment Center designed to established benchmarks for testing the potential for future management candidates, I was selected as one of ten supervisors company-wide, to help set the standards by which future candidates would be judged. My immediate supervisor confided to me that he had suggested I was not a good choice, as I would tend to raise the standards too high for most people to meet. Please believe me, I do not mention these things to brag! At this point in my life, who'd care anyway? I am only trying to relay the message of how perilously prone we impulsive and reckless-abandon people are to foot shooting. Also, it is important to relay my total preoccupation with work and gradual drifting away from the all-important family side of our lives. In spite of the fact that DeAnn and I were joining Jaycees, bridge clubs, bowling leagues, and many other social functions together, I was seeing all this socializing as a means to my gain rather than an enjoyable joint effort by DeAnn and myself. DeAnn probably did not realize just how much my personal life had married itself to my professional life until we had our first annual awards banquet for my group, held at the largest restaurant in town. My boss and his wife, his boss and his wife, and all my employees and the other supervisors' employees and their wives were in attendance. I served as master of ceremonies and felt everything went very well. On the ride home I was feeling extremely self-satisfied.

"How long has your secretary been in love with you?" DeAnn asked in a matter of fact way.

"What secretary?" I was truly puzzled.

"Oh come on! She hung on and repeated nearly every word you uttered tonight! When you singled her out as 'the most wonderful secretary in the world' she almost swooned." She had me there.

To be sure, my personal secretary, Jewel, was nearly as perfect as a secretary could be. I could ask her to make certain I did not miss a meeting six months in advance and not have to worry about it anymore. In fact, she had helped write most of my speeches that evening. She was an invaluable tool who always managed to sense the oncoming frustrations of my employees and alert me in time to head off problems. She willingly kept daily vigilance of my budget and never tired of keeping me up-to-date. However, I was so preoccupied with my own career advancement I had not even noticed her personal attraction to me. I was ignoring her "love" as much as my homelife.

Apparently, Jewel's husband was as perceptive as DeAnn had been at the banquet. The following Monday morning I received a severe jolt. "I realize this will probably not affect you one way or the other," Jewel opened the morning dialogue. "I am resigning from this job. Please consider this my two-week notice."

"Why, and what makes you say it won't affect me one way or the other?" I stammered.

"Well, first of all, you only look at me as another piece of furniture around here. That's why I know it won't matter to you one way or another. Second, I had a very passionate dream last night and called out your name in it! Needless to say, my husband did not appreciate that. He told me I must resign today! So, what do *you* want me to do?"

"I suppose you would not believe me if I said I cannot live without you," I stupidly replied.

"Does that mean you are in love with me?" she asked breathlessly.

"I suppose it does," I responded, immediately hating myself for saying it.

While driving home that evening, I beat myself to death. God, I must tell DeAnn about this. But how? I could not live with this load of guilt. Running through my mind was, "Do I really love this woman?" My conclusion was that I did, but as a sister. No, a little more than that. As a lover? Yes, but not enough to betray my wife.

Entering the door I immediately sensed that my old confidant already knew my thoughts. I confessed the loss of my secretary was probably going to make it impossible for me to do my job. I just could not think of doing without her. To my surprise, DeAnn expressed understanding. I was a little puzzled by her apparent understanding, but later supposed it was because she had also been a little infatuated with her first boss, something I sensed at the time but had never been quite willing to acknowledge.

My marriage and my career, from my perspective, were both on idyllic paths. I was madly in love with my pregnant wife. So why in hell did I fall into a stupid, although temporary and fleeting infatuation? Pity? Certainly this beautiful, intelligent, sexy blonde secretary did not need pity! So why did I not just walk away and let her alone? Who knows?

In the end, following a late-night visit to our door by Jewel's husband with a gun in his hand, I concluded the only solution was to run! Fear was not the motivation. Well, not *all* of the motivation. This unexpected visit had been skillfully turned into a positive rather than negative situation by DeAnn. She answered the door and convinced the guy to pocket his firearm before entering by telling him she already knew all about the "love affair." She suggested it was already ended and that the three of us sit down and discuss the solution to our mutual problem. Her approach so deflated the fellow that he broke down in tears and began to confess how he was probably partly to blame himself. He had been ignoring his wife due to work commitments and she had sought solace from me. Guilt started to wrench at my gut. If he loved her this much why was I messing around with her affections? An even better question was why was I messing around with DeAnn's affections this way?

The following week I got together with my boss and requested his help in getting a transfer…anywhere. The eleventh floor in downtown Cleveland was offered. The company even agreed to pay for our move to a new home. DeAnn and I decided to purchase my family beach home on the shores of Lake Erie and AT&T moved us back to our hometown. I began to commute to Cleveland every day.

During those last five years, I had become the youngest "in charge" technician and the youngest first-level supervisor in the Cleveland District. In addition to the Management Assessment Center honor, I was also one of the first training instructors at the new AT&T Campus in Cincinnati. Now I was to become the youngest eleventh-floor Private Line Services Supervisor ever at 750 Huron. These accolades, along with all the other special treatment I had received from AT&T, should have assured my making them my permanent home. Maybe it should have. However, I did not enjoy working in downtown Cleveland. I did not enjoy the prospect of working in downtown Chicago and New York City, as was predicted to be my career path by "people in the know." Most of all, I did not enjoy spending so much of my time away from my home and family required by commuting and constant out-of-town assignments.

Professionally, what I yearned for was to become a part of the fledgling satellite communications field being pioneered by AT&T. These were the early days of satellite communications. Russia had launched "Sputnik" and we had responded with our "Early Bird." AT&T was building huge impressive satellite ground antenna stations on the East and West Coasts. I read every article printed about satellites, which fascinated me to the point of an obsession. Also, the new states of Alaska and Hawaii were natural areas for satellite installations. Alaska fascinated me even more than the idea of being a part of the new ability to use outer space technology to instantly communicate around the world. To my mind the potential was unlimited, which certainly proved to be true.

I kept pestering my new boss in Cleveland to recommend me for any position at one of the new earth station installations. He would not. In fact, he informed me I was going nowhere until he got promoted himself. I went over his head to his boss, which made both of them unhappy. I went over both of their heads to the area plant manager, which made *everybody* unhappy. We took a vacation and visited the earth station sites and tried to get myself transferred to one of them on their recommendation. This was not a good idea! I was acting in a very impulsive and reckless manner in a large conservative company with a well-established chain of command. This current obsession of mine was not only raising havoc with my job performance, it was affecting our homelife as well. I felt a new direction in my life was called for.

Both knowing what was undoubtedly on the horizon, with my urging, DeAnn began taking classes to obtain a real estate license. We were preparing in advance for my becoming temporarily unemployed. She passed the exam and interviewed with the person everyone she talked to called the most knowledgeable, but also the most demanding broker in the area. This demanding broker, Walter Witt, insisted she give him a resume including a letter explaining to him, in detail, just what she could do for his company. She panicked a little at this but wrote the letter. He was so impressed that he not only hired her, he framed the letter and hung it behind the desk in his office. Over the next few months he took her under his wing and personally trained her for her new career. The stage was now set for *my* career change with the least amount of financial pain possible, I was convincing myself.

After making a final series of requests to be assigned to a satellite earth station, with the same negative results as the previous attempts, I resigned from AT&T. Poor DeAnn, who never really believed I would throw away the job of the century, was certain our world had come to an end. We now had five children and I was out of work.

CHAPTER 4

# The Ranch:

## *Desperately in Search of Change*

*Changes begun in* desperation rarely work out as planned.

It seemed I was not the only family member looking for a drastic change at this point in time. Shortly after my resignation from AT&T, DeAnn's family gathered for a reunion at our home on Lake Erie. Her younger sister Amy and husband Richard came from California. They were as fed up with California and their jobs at Hughes Aircraft Company as I had become with AT&T and commuting to Cleveland. At the reunion, Amy, Richard, and I decided the answer was to "drop out of society" and go into partnership on a ranch out west. Idaho or Montana seemed to be the best choice for us. We persuaded DeAnn to join us on a trip west to go ranch hunting.

Over a period of several weeks we looked at every ranch for sale in northern Idaho and western Montana. We finally settled on the Gold Creek ranch near Potomac, Montana, just twenty miles

**Home on Lake Erie in Ohio.**

east of Missoula. Although located in a pristine setting, the ranch did not lend itself to the promise of an "independent survival" situation. It did show great possibilities as a dude ranch. The four of us had lengthy discussions concerning our game plan. The consensus reached, as DeAnn and I heard it, was that Richard would obtain a Montana guide license to take hunting clients into the adjacent Bob Marshall Wilderness area and I would manage the cabin and lodge remodeling to handle dude ranch guests. We

Montana ranch house.

parted company after agreeing to put the profit from the sale of our homes, predicted to be equal, into the ranch.

God sometimes has a strange way of intervening in your plans. On our return to Ohio we were greeted with the news that a slimy little bunch of bikers calling themselves the "Hell's Angels" had invaded our little village and were terrorizing this formerly peaceful little family resort. They were, in fact, camped on the beach below our home when we returned late at night. Never being bashful, I emptied my 12-gauge shotgun over their heads. Followed by screaming expletives, was the sound of bikes spinning in the sand. No more bikers.

As if the Hell's Angels, or whoever they were, wasn't troubling enough, the opening of the St. Lawrence Seaway raised the level of Lake Erie several feet. During the following year several feet of earth and many trees on the 200-foot lake bank between our home and the shoreline disappeared. Over the next ten years, the cottage and garage located between the house and the lake were to be claimed by the elevated lake level. As property all along the lakefront began eroding, our lakefront mansion became unmarketable. Those not afraid of the bikers returning were scared to death of losing their homes to the lake. To further complicate an already tenuous situation, Amy and Richard sold their home immediately and were in the process of packing to head for Montana. And I was still out of work! Could anything else go wrong?

Going job hunting after just having quit a position any sane person in the world considered a job to kill for is *not* a recommended course of action. Every personnel manager had the same stock answer for not hiring me. "You wouldn't be happy here. We could never pay you as much as AT&T had." Although never spoken, these statements actually translated to, "If you weren't happy there you certainly wouldn't be happy here!"

I decided the communications field had been a big mistake.

My father-in-law found a temporary job for me as a house painter. I was *fired* after two days for being too slow as I took great pains, at the owner's insistence, to cover all of the beautiful flower gardens all around the house so as not to splatter paint on them. This really helped my already deflated ego!

My father, overjoyed that we had returned to our hometown, was now in the process of buying up old homes, remodeling them, and turning them into rental units. He took pity on us and hired me to do electrical and plumbing upgrades on these units. This job with my father allowed me to apply for lower paying jobs, requiring no resume.

With references from my father and father-in-law, I was finally able to land a job building camper trailers. Having the electrical and plumbing background helped. This job paid about one third what I had been making with AT&T, but it was a start…or something.

The camper job lasted about six months before they declared bankruptcy. Meanwhile, DeAnn and I moved our seven-member family from our five bedroom home, which had always been called the "mansion" by my brothers and our children, to a small two-bedroom guest cottage located on the property. We then rented out the mansion in an attempt to cut expenses. God, I love her!

Finally, a small break came our way. An old friend of mine from AT&T told me about a position opening at Reliance Electric, a large manufacturer of electric motors and motor control components near our home. I applied. The personnel manager was understandably leery about hiring someone with my background. He made me sign a one-year commitment and agreement to train other new hires to work as assembly line quality control inspectors, on an evening shift. This position paid no more than the camper trailer job but was not very demanding, which left me free to do some daytime moonlighting carpenter work for my father and plumbing work for my father-in-law on weekends. The nondemanding job also gave me some time to reflect on the past year since shooting myself in the foot with AT&T. I was wallowing in regret!

Almost two years after the bikers incident, mostly because of horrendous erosion problems, the lakefront property was still not selling and our partners were now firmly entrenched on the ranch. DeAnn and I borrowed the money from a finance company to make our half of the ranch payments. Disenchantment with the ranch was setting in when DeAnn and I decided to go out to Montana for a visit. The welcome by our "partners" was, to put it mildly, cool. They showed no sympathy for our inability to sell our property on Lake Erie. The sad facts were that Richard and I had both been seeking to become "independent" and get far away from society and control of our lives by others. We *both* had the same goal, which was to control our own lives. In a partnership between two equally stubborn, pigheaded guys such as Richard and me neither of us would have the independence each wanted most in life. Failure was inevitable. Upon returning to Ohio, much to our lawyer's dismay, we signed our half of the ranch over to Amy and Richard.

DeAnn was secretly overjoyed. I was a little relieved myself.

# CHAPTER 5

# The Satellite Communications Field Finally Welcomes Me

*Fate definitely has a* way of interceding. Put another way, when God closes a door he always leaves a window open. I guess this holds true even if you are the one who closed the door. As chance would have it, in early 1968, Reliance Electric received an order to make some antenna drive motors for a satellite communications company based in Washington, DC. As predicted at one of the AT&T seminars I had attended in 1965, against all odds, the communications giant did lose the satellite business to the government-supported private corporation named Communications Satellite Corporation (COMSAT).

I began to scan the want ads in all the major newspapers. The *Cleveland Plain Dealer* was advertising for technicians in the "new and exciting" satellite communications field. I searched for the name on the order for drive motors. It was COMSAT. I called the number in the ad. They said to mail a resume. A week went by with no response so I called again and asked for the personnel manager. He also told me to mail a resume. He volunteered that this was the last day of interviews and all positions had probably been filled. I refused to be put off, and gave him a quick synopsis of my background. To my surprise and delight he nearly shouted, "Wait a minute, I think I know you! My name is Jack Williams and I attended the assessment center for AT&T at the same time you did. I have often wondered whatever happened to you."

"See here," he added. "I will call the recruiters in Cleveland and, if they are willing and you can be there this evening, I'll ask them to meet with you."

I assured him I would be there in no more than three hours. I did not tell him it was a two-hour drive, of course. I grabbed a copy of my resume, dressed in my best suit, said a prayer, asked DeAnn to say several prayers, and headed for Cleveland. She called my boss at Reliance and told him I would not be in that evening.

The COMSAT interview was conducted by three very earnest gentlemen who were all rapidly firing questions at me concerning every detail of my past employment history. The money being offered was less than half the salary AT&T had paid but I would have paid *them* for a chance at this position. I think they sensed that. I really didn't care. In the back of my mind was to just get the job. Then, when they realized how valuable I was, we could rectify the salary and benefit portion.

I did, however, have the presence of mind to make one request. When they started a site in Alaska, I wanted to go there. They informed me they had no such plan. I insisted, "Will you please note in my file, if hired, I would like to be considered for relocating to Alaska if a site is built there?"

"Why not?" one of them made a note, "If we go to Alaska, I am certain we will need all the volunteers we can get."

The final question put to me was, "We have sites going into Puerto Rico, Hawaii, California, New Jersey, and West Virginia. What would your choice be in descending order?"

"Hawaii, California, Puerto Rico, New Jersey, West Virginia."

West Virginia, here we come! Oh well, no plan is perfect.

CHAPTER 6

# West Virginia:
## *Strangers in a Strange Land*

*I must say we spent* two very pleasant years in West Virginia. We made some of our best friends in the world there. Though DeAnn was forced to put her real estate career on hold, our social life was nothing but pleasant.

However, DeAnn's introduction to West Virginia was a little less than splendid. The new "science fiction era" COMSAT Etam earth station was located in one of the most improbable locations on earth. We were dropped in the middle of a "radio quiet" zone that still lived in the 1930s. The location was the—uncivilized by our standards—Cheat Mountain area of West Virginia. The area immediately surrounding the earth station was inhabited by slightly less than stable people who hung out on the main street, offering a kind of slack-jawed greeting to all cars passing through the small village. The one hundred or so people associated with new earth station personnel and families were probably the only new inhabitants to occupy the area since the Civil War.

Being kind, I will say this scared the hell out of DeAnn! Not realizing my ultimate goal was Alaska at any cost, she had the initial impression this move to West Virginia was some sort of punishment I was inflicting upon her. I was determined to concentrate only on enhancing my career, once again, by utilizing this "temporary" tour in West Virginia as the key to Alaska. I was not all that worried about her feelings.

We temporarily left the children with grandparents in Ohio while the company paid for DeAnn and me to stay at the only motel in Parsons. DeAnn concentrated her efforts on finding us a suitable home to rent. I concentrated on my new career. The outgoing and intuitive DeAnn easily made friends with Evy, the county clerk of courts, while checking out the West Virginia requirements to obtain driver's licenses. Evy informed her of the possibility of renting an old Victorian home under her charge, pending an estate settlement. The two of them arranged for Evy and her husband Elroy to meet us at the large home located in Holly Meadows.

We approached the monstrous three-story old Victorian entirely overgrown with hemlock, holly, and blackberry vines. The old stone wall and wrought iron gate across the front yard entrance were covered with climbing rose bushes long ago gone wild. The front entrance oak-and-stained-glass door was locked solid and they had no key. We beat our way through the underbrush and up the rickety back steps to an unlocked rear entrance with an old-style "skeleton key" lock. We pushed the sagging door across the rotting floor and carefully entered. To the right was a large depression-era kitchen. The old wooden sink was still mounted in the worn, curled linoleum countertop. The hole where a hand water pump had once been mounted was still visible. An old set of cast-iron faucets was held in place above the sink by the cast-iron pipes and several bent nails. There were no cabinets. The ancient linoleum floor had been laid over tongue-and-groove flooring, which had long ago separated and broken the linoleum at each groove. To the left of the rear entrance was what had once been a sitting room. A previous tenant had decided to store apples from the old fruit trees surrounding the home in the sitting room. The smell of rotting apples piled waist-deep on the once beautiful oak floors filled the air. Several rats scurried into hiding as we entered.

A large squeaky swinging door allowed entrance from the kitchen to the formal dining room. A previous tenant had turned this once gorgeous dining room into a coal bin! The oak flooring was heaped with coal chunks beside a pot-bellied stove. The vent for the stove was inserted through a hole that once contained a small windowpane. The stove was located on a mammoth tile hearth in front of what once had been a lovely oak-faced fireplace. The oak fireplace finish had been scorched and split beyond repair by years of abusive overheating from the stove.

Between the apple-storing sitting room and a large living room was a set of solid cherry pocket doors. Both the sitting room and the living room had oak-and-tile-faced fireplaces similar to the one in the dining room. We worked our way around to the main entrance. A large transom door accessed the main hallway from both the dining room and the living room. An ornate oak banister stairway wound to the second floor balcony. Off the balcony, through more ornate transom doors, were four large bedrooms. An old hall closet at the top of the stairs had been converted to a makeshift bathroom with a cast-iron stationary tub, a rusty old sink, and a toilet with an overhead pull-chain flush tank. Two of the bedrooms also had fireplaces. The old wallpaper had separated from the lath plaster in many places and hung at grotesque angles around the rooms. A couple of bats flew up the fireplace as we entered one of the bedrooms. Every room had at least one small glass pane broken or missing from the old multipaned double-hung windows.

The wooden ceiling laths were protruding through the plaster in many places, indicating roof leaks. Observing my obvious concern, the clerk volunteered that the roof had been completely replaced a year ago. I continued to climb a second open oak stairway to the third floor, to be greeted by a slightly foreboding door.

"Just the attic up thar," the clerk called out.

I wanted to see if any recent roof leaks were evident in the attic. Her husband sensed this and smiled approvingly. The "attic" was another full story composed of two 16' x 20' plastered and wallpapered rooms with large gabled windows through which a few more bats exited as we entered. We found no evidence of *recent* leaks.

As we descended the stairs, DeAnn asked how the place was heated, other than the intolerable coal stove. Elroy informed her that natural gas was plumbed to the hot water tank and the kitchen. A furnace could easily be added, but was not in the estate budget. "Doesn't get all that cold he-ar in winter. Lots of fareplaces. Some of 'em haive gas plumbed to 'em."

"Where are the well and septic located?" I asked.

Elroy showed a small glint of admiration that I had assumed there would be well and septic rather than city water and sewer.

22

"Cribs out baiik and still works probably," he shrugged. "No guaranty on thaait I'm affeared. Well's in front of hewouse. Show it to yew'all on the way aieout. Pumps in cellear. Tried to get it goin' layeest week. Some problem. Yew'all know enythin' bought pumps?"

"Suure due," I assured him trying to get into his dialect.

"Leeits go take a look see," he motioned me to a rickety door off the kitchen pantry.

He turned the old rotating porcelain light switch causing a bare lightbulb to blink on at the foot of the nearly vertical wooden stairs. We heard a rustle like leaves in the wind as the light came on. An old farm boy like me recognized this as more rats!

The rusty well pump was located in a far corner. The pressure switch was plugged into an adapter screwed into a former light socket via an extension cord. Elroy plugged the cord into the adapter and nothing happened. I excused myself and went upstairs to find a lightbulb, returned, and unscrewed the adapter from the socket. I screwed the bulb into the socket and it lit. Elroy frowned and gave a little shrug indicating he had already tried this himself. I then reached over and hit the pressure switch with my knuckle. It clicked and hummed but nothing else happened. Unplugging the extension cord, I removed the pressure switch cover. It was full of rust and corrosion. I reached into my pocket for my ever-present jackknife. After using the knife to burnish the switch contacts, I then slightly loosened the pressure control screw. Upon plugging the extension cord back into the adapter, the pump began to whirl.

"By gawd, yawl do know pumps!" Elroy exclaimed.

As the pipes in the house clattered and banged, we headed for the top floor to open the old faucets on the bathroom sink. After several minutes, we still had no water.

"Ell...roy, yawl got water up thar?" We heard the clerk yell from the kitchen.

"Ain't a speck yer!" he shouted back.

"Got a lot down here!" DeAnn screamed.

23

We rushed downstairs to the sight of water raining through the kitchen ceiling. "Must be a-leakin'," Elroy made the understatement of the day. He scurried down to unplug the pump.

DeAnn and Evy began a final run through the house to shut off all lights and we left via the old rear door. Elroy took me to locate the well and septic.

DeAnn and Evy remained on the old back porch watching the waning evening sun forming long shadows behind the old barn, henhouse, and hay meadows framed by the mountains behind the house.

Elroy cautiously removed the lid from the hand-dug well. There were several frogs jumping around on the rock walls and two or three dead rats floating in the water. A black snake or two scurried into holes between the rock walls.

"Uh-huh," I winked. "Don't mention the rats and snakes to DeAnn, okay?"

He held an index finger to his lips and gave an impish little shake of his head.

"Is there a spring for drinking water nearby?" I asked.

"Might check with them thar Hiles next door," he pointed to the farmhouse down the road.

As we replaced the well cover, De and Evy approached. "I know you Yankee folk probably ain't interested in this 'ere old Smith place but *ai* love it so much *ai* just hayed to show it to y'all." She gave a motherly look to DeAnn. "Jus' gotta show y'all one more thing 'fore we all leave."

We all followed Evy as she crossed the road and ascended a well-worn path to the top of a small ridge looking westerly. The sun was setting over a wide, slowly drifting river turning majestically golden. "The Cheat," she murmured. After a long pause to take in the beauty of the scene, we strolled back to the darkening and slightly foreboding ghost-like Victorian mansion as the sun dropped below the town beyond the river. "Ahi sposes y'all ain't intrested, but with your big famly this place could be made a home. Need some rent, but might make it easy for the rait famly. Maybe fifty dollars a month to cover court administration costs."

Receiving no immediate response from us, she added, "Spose not." As she turned to go.

"We love it," DeAnn and I chorused. "You have a deal!"

It was obvious she wanted to hug us but restrained herself.

As I was already working full-time overseeing equipment installations and training new personnel, DeAnn was forced to make the three-hundred-mile round-trip to retrieve our sons Carl and Lee. I was going to need their help if we were to ever get the Victorian ready to live in.

While DeAnn returned to Ohio to retrieve the three younger children from her mother, the older boys and I were kept busy, working into the late hours repairing plumbing, wiring, and windowpanes, and shoveling apples and coal from the house.

The boys, now approaching teen age, and I spent many hours together sanding and varnishing oak floors, patching plaster, and hanging wallpaper to restore the old dinosaur to at least a shadow of its former self. During the days, while I was working at COMSAT, they also trimmed back the thorny undergrowth around the house and mowed a lawn that hadn't seen a mower in years. The snapping turtles, copperheads, and black snakes weren't very happy about that!

West Virginia Victorian.

We repaired the old chicken coop, made it as rat-proof as possible, and filled it with bantam chicks.

The boys and I spent more time together that summer than any other time in our lives. It was a joy for me! They also have reminded me many times over the years how much they learned at my side during this time.

We were all very happy to see DeAnn, Jeannie, D'Aun, and little Patrick return with DeAnn's parents. More welcome help!

COMSAT was becoming anxious to see us off their hotel bill and into our own residence.

Fall arrived and school started.

To say the least, DeAnn was not happy with the West Virginia school system. After a period of a few months the local principal would dive out his office window whenever he heard her little high heels click-clacking down the hall toward his office.

DeAnn really went on a rampage upon discovering our oldest daughter Jeannie was constantly ill from being seated in line with the hot air register spewing coal gas fumes from the ancient furnace. After the daughter of one of our new friends was nearly drowned by the janitor, washing down the restroom with a fire hose, DeAnn gained a valuable homeborn ally to join in the fight.

She helped organize a group of the local mothers to start a preschool/kindergarden program. The principal agreed they could turn an old coal bin room into a classroom. It was no easy task, but these energetic women scrubbed down and painted this filthy basement room. Now all they needed was a teacher.

The parents paid to send their kids to this preschool/kindergarten. The fees also paid for a certified teacher. Thus was born the first preschool program in Parsons.

As president of the newly formed Jayceettes, DeAnn enlisted me, as legislative affairs chairman of the Jaycees, to help push through an unprecedented real estate tax increase ballot initiative to help shore up the school budget, last increased in the 1940s. The Jaycee president and I managed to ignite enough enthusiasm to canvas the area and ask every voter to support the issue. A local "good ole boy" was paired with me. His first warning was to tell me if we approached a house and the porch light went out we should, "Hit the dirt 'cause he's tak'n a bead on yew." When this would happen, as it often did, he would shout out to the household, "This here's Billy Bob Lee, Efrom's boy."

"Hell's bells, come on in boy," was a typical answer as the light came back on. We would go in and present our case for the little tax increase.

None of us, including the local Jaycees, truly realized at the time just how the caste society was still in control of this backwoods part of West Virginia. We were ministering to the choir. A choir that agreed with us in principle but bent to the will of their landlords at the ballot box. Landlords who followed upon our heels to inform their tenants the rent would increase to allow for our (greatly exaggerated by them) proposed tax increase.

Any mil rate in that county required a 55 percent vote. As I now reflect, not really a bad idea. We managed about 51 percent on the ballot. It came closer to passing than ever before.

For better or worse, we eventually used this bad school system as one of the reasons for eventually leaving West Virginia. The schools in 1967 West Virginia were underfunded on facilities but had teachers who at least attempted to teach the basics while maintaining a discipline tempered with common sense. The older teachers were there because they wanted to be in the profession of teaching children. The younger teachers were there because they had left the area to get a degree and had returned to help the struggling school system. They certainly were not there for the pay, which averaged about two to three thousand dollars per year. Even my meager COMSAT salary was more than twice that. Drug problems certainly were nonexistent. Who could afford them? In retrospect, were our children really better served by leaving this?

In early spring of our second year we asked Mr. Hile on the farm next door if he would plow the field south of the house for a garden. "Well, I guess so," he drawled. "It used to be a hog lot, probably ain't too good for a garden." The logic of this entirely escaped me! As an old farm boy I felt a vacated hog lot would be a great garden spot.

The garden proved to be a showplace. We entered gigantic beets, zucchini, peppers, tomatoes, string beans, and popcorn in the county fair that year and won first place ribbons on all. A disappointment was our 100-pound pumpkin. We learned that the pumpkin contest was annually the most competitive at the fair. The winner was well over 200 pounds!

By fall of that second year we had completely refinished all of the now beautiful oak floors, interior doors, ornate woodwork, and fireplaces. We refurbished the huge entryway brass chandelier and enhanced the entry with red-and-white flocked wallpaper. The formal dining room we papered with green-and-white flocked. The sitting and living rooms we painted a rich cream and adorned the windows with huge blue-and-gold drapes with sheer drop curtains.

The budget was tight because the lakefront home in Ohio had still not sold. With the help of our Sears credit card, auction sales, garage sales, and a small loan from Dad we were able to obtain oak dining room furniture and Victorian chairs and lounges throughout the house.

We borrowed my dad's table saw and purchased several sheets of birch plywood with which we proceeded to build a country-style kitchen.

The home had recently been painted outside, thank God! We added window flower boxes and several hanging baskets of fuchsias and begonia along the over-fifty-feet-long front and side porches. The boys and I manicured the lawns and massive rose bushes, privet hedges, and juniper to perfection.

Restoration of the beautiful Victorian became a labor of love for all of us.

Word of our labors spread throughout the valley. Almost daily, slow-moving vehicles ventured down Holly Meadows Lane to observe firsthand the gradual remodeling of the old Smith Victorian by the *Yankees*.

To DeAnn's surprise and delight, Evy and an elderly lady calling herself Mrs. Smith appeared at the front door one afternoon. Mrs. Smith informed De that she had been brought to this home as a bride. She wondered if she might come in and look around.

She and Evy were both amazed to find that many of the colors and designs we had used with paint and wallpaper were very similar to the original. The carpet runner that covered the open stairway to the top floor was the same carpet she had put in forty years ago. She was, however, appalled that the beautiful oak fireplace in the dining room had been painted. DeAnn explained how the oak had been so badly damaged when a previous tenant had use it with a coal-fired heating unit, so painting it was the best solution. Mrs. Smith tried to understand but was obviously disappointed.

After joining De in a cup of tea, Mrs. Smith, leaning on Evy's arm, tearfully and somewhat reluctantly departed, thanking De for being so kind and gracious.

The Victorian being so beautifully restored and also located on one of the best "swimmin' holes" in the area, naturally became a fun party house for our newfound friends and their kids. On summer days the kids all filled the "swimmin' hole" to overflowing.

Halloween parties became our big specialty. Our Jaycee couples and many of the couples from the COMSAT site delighted in coming to our "haunted house" parties, for which the big old Victorian was a natural setting.

Christmas in West Virginia.

# CHAPTER 7

# The Colonel

*The Etam earth station* was, like all the original COMSAT earth stations, designed and run by a group of retired military communications personnel. Although efficient in their minds, the military regimen seemed unnecessary at times and, indeed, rather laughable to most of the newly hired technicians like myself who had very little military background.

The "Colonel," who served as the Etam site manager, required everyone to wear an ID badge with his name and title on it. This badge must be shown to the guard at the locked entrance gate in order to report to work. It must be worn in full view at all times while on the site. No excuse for not prominently displaying your badge at all times was acceptable.

At payday all personnel lined up at the Colonel's office door. Each technician was admitted, one at a time, to receive a full "dress-down" concerning all mistakes made over the past two weeks. During the first two months at least one tech every week stormed from the Colonel's office, issued a few ill-chosen expletives, slammed the door behind him, and disappeared, never to be seen again. An old technician named Bill Bell, with whom I had become quite friendly, and I had begun to take bets on who would be next to "go over the wall." Additionally, we had started growing beards, which we knew would irk the Colonel to no end.

The infernal ID badge was forever getting caught on equipment racks or wires when working in tight places. I had developed the habit of inserting the badge in my shirt vest pocket so as not to lose it. On about the fifth or sixth payday everyone was lined up at the Colonel's door. As I went to enter, one of the site supervisors reminded me my badge was not properly displayed. Being in a rather bad mood that day I responded, "Oh, sorry," as I pinned the badge to my fly upon entering the Colonel's office.

"Boy!" the Colonel roared. "That badge deserves more respect than that. Display it properly and do not ever pull this kind of tomfoolery again!"

"Oh come on, Bill, knock it off. Where's your sense of humor?" I addressed the Colonel by his first name, also a breach of protocol. "How the hell many people do you have to run off with this silly, military bullshit before it dawns on you that you are now in a *civilian* job?"

"That will do, young man!"

"I'm sorry, Bill, but it will not do. I'm getting a little tired of training good people out there just to have you run them off with your silly rules." I extended my hand for what I was certain would be my final COMSAT paycheck.

"Get back to work, son," he stood and handed me my check.

"Yes, sir!" I shouted as I saluted, spun on my heels and goose-stepped toward the door.

"Hold it!" He shouted. As I was turning the doorknob he added, "Please?"

That stopped me.

"Carl, please sit down." He also sat. He then leaned back in his swivel chair and heaved a sigh.

"It sounds to me as though you're telling me I have been acting pretty much like an ass."

"You said it, not me."

"Keep an eye on me. If I don't improve, let me know. Be a little more kind next time though, will you?"

"That's a promise, sir."

As I exited his office the entire line of people grasped my hand and about shook it off. Old Bill Bell was doubled up in a corner laughing so hard he could barely speak. "You are one gutsy SOB," he managed to croak as I passed. Obviously the door to the Colonel's office was not soundproof.

The site working conditions did improve somewhat. For one, the site supervisors each passed the payroll checks to their group from that day forward. My respect for the Colonel improved dramatically. I still kept the beard though.

As for my professional advancement in West Virginia, I quickly learned my limited knowledge of satellite systems was not what had gotten me the position. It was my knowledge of the telephone company industry. I could speak "telephoneze" with the local connecting telephone companies. In other words, if we were right and they were wrong, I could help prove it! Most of my first few months were spent training our technicians to work on the equipment interfacing to AT&T. Meanwhile, I worked hard to become the most informed technician on the satellite side of the system. Making myself the site expert on all systems, I was always in demand during panic situations, of which there were many in those early days.

Being able to speak and interpret French was also a plus when the snotty French decided to converse with us only in French rather than the recognized international language of English.

All of this notoriety eventually led to a request for me to transfer to Washington, DC, to become the official training instructor for the company. My first training assignment was to be Alaska. Arranging a meeting with Jack Williams, I reminded him of my request to transfer to Alaska if we had a site there. He promised me I would not like Alaska well enough to stay. He informed me the site was in a remote area halfway between Anchorage and Fairbanks. There were only two hundred people in the whole town (about the size of the community I grew up in). The road to the site was just now being built. Until now, it had been accessed by rail or air. It was primitive by his standards. All this only whet my appetite. "If I like it, can I stay?"

"If you like it, we only have a senior technician slot open," was his answer.

"Fine."

"You won't like it!" my New York–native boss chided.

Upon hearing my request, the new Alaska site manager, Bill Punderson, traveled to Etam to meet with me. I invited him to dinner at our home. He spent most of the evening expressing his joy concerning my wanting to join his Alaskan force. We also discussed my Alaska salary. It was agreed that because I had been increased to mid-level senior technician pay in Etam he would honor that equivalent salary in Alaska. He stated that the senior technician range was to be $300 to $400 per week. We shook hands and I promised to arrive in Alaska the first week of April 1970, after spending three months in DC preparing lesson plans for COMSAT.

DeAnn was *not* happy. I suspect she stayed with me through the resignation from AT&T, the move to West Virginia, and the possibility of moving to DC simply out of sheer grit and stubborn Russian determination. But, leaving our gracious newly restored mansion and moving to an unknown, undefined, and *unwanted* life in Alaska was the last straw!

For better or worse, my mother-in-law came to my rescue. This normally soft-spoken, God-loving, and unassuming woman, who had always made a strict practice of never interfering in our marriage, spoke up in support of Alaska.

When Punderson and I dropped the Alaska bomb on DeAnn, her mother and father were visiting us. As soon as Punderson left our home, DeAnn stormed to our bedroom sobbing uncontrollably. She slammed the door closed and threw herself on the bed to have a good cry.

Not being able to ignore this most unusual show of temper from her oldest daughter, DeAnn's dear mom hurried to the bedroom door and tapped lightly, "DeAnn, is that you crying? What is the problem, child? May I come in?" Only more sobbing was her answer.

Her mother slowly opened the door and entered to sit on the bed beside her distraught daughter. DeAnn threw herself into her mother's arms. "He wants to move to *Alaska!*"

"Is that all?" Her mother heaved a sigh of relief. "My goodness, what an adventure that will be!"

"But, Mom, *why Alaska?*"

CHAPTER 8

# Alaska or Bust!

*On to Alaska.* Impulsive and reckless? Well…maybe…maybe not.

DeAnn and I did not move to Alaska together. With my promising Punderson to be on the site by April First (*April Fool?!*) DeAnn had been forced to remain behind to allow the children to finish the school year and supervise the packing of our belongings for shipment to Alaska. Our number-two son Lee, being almost twelve and trying to become too much of a problem for his mother, went with me.

We drove my pickup truck to Seattle and put it on a barge to Anchorage. We then flew to Alaska. This trip allowed me to hold him as a captive audience for some lengthy discussions about his little attitude problems. The outcome being that he and I probably identified as soul brothers for years afterward. Hey, ain't that great!

A crazy man, named Karl Whelm, met us at the Anchorage airport. Whelm had been hired by COMSAT as a site mechanic. Fortunately, he was driving a 4WD International pickup. Without this vehicle we would never have made the drive over the muddy road, mostly without any bridges, to Talkeetna, Alaska. This long drive (more than 120 miles) was our introduction to Alasaka's "spring breakup."

The site construction people, Karl, and Punderson were all staying at the only hotel in town, a place called Evil Alice's. Our first big disappointment was not long in coming. Evil Alice did not allow kids in her hotel. She recommended Lee and I try to find a room at the old log Roadhouse. She looked me straight in the eye with her tiny boney five-foot-tall frame by grabbing my lapel and pulling my nose right down to hers. " Do not tell Caroll or Verna I sent you to the Roadhouse," she demanded.

Karl and I loaded our bags and Lee into his truck and headed around the corner to the Roadhouse. "Watch your step in here, " Karl warned. "These people are strange. No profanity! I'll wait out here with your bags."

"What in the hell have we gotten into?" I was thinking to myself. A scrawny little old lady had just threatened to punch my lights out and now we were having to beg for a room from some "strange" people. What next?

We cautiously opened the Roadhouse door, which tripped a bell hanging at just the right level to be rung by the top edge of the swinging door. A boney little old man in baggy army surplus khaki pants and a white T-shirt was poking small pieces of wood into a stove next to a doorway about twenty feet behind an old lunch counter. Along the counter were several well-worn revolving stools. Very reminiscent of the bar stools in a 1950s-era drugstore.

"If you're looking for food, can't help you," the old guy croaked around a cigarette stuck to the corner of his mouth as he closed the stove top using his apron as a hot pad.

"We were hoping to get a room, if possible," I managed while wondering to myself whatever happened to hello?

"Just you and the boy?" He began to amble to the counter.

"Yes."

"Just for the night?" He laid both elbows on the counter directly beneath the "No Smoking" sign. "Go ahead and sit."

We obeyed. "No," I managed a smile, " probably for a month or more. My Name is Carl and this is my son Lee."

"How old you, son?" He shook Lee's hand.

"Almost twelve."

"Where's your mom?"

"She and my brothers and sisters are still in West Virginia until they finish school," Lee volunteered.

"West Virginia, eh?" He glanced at me. "You don't go to school?" He began to toy with Lee's mind.

"My dad is going to put me in school here...."

35

"What makes you so special? You your dad's favorite or something?" More little mind games.

"Must be," Lee looked at me and fidgeted a little in his seat.

"Five kids, eh? Your wife sure has her hands full!" he finally decided to include me in the conversation. "So you want a room. Suppose you want to see it first."

"I'm sure it will be okay. We don't need to see it first."

"Good thing! If you wanted to see it first, no room," he winked. "Fellow feels he can't trust me don't stay here! It'll be $50 a day and you share a bathroom with everybody else. Place is locked up tight at ten o'clock. If you're not in, you're locked out. No smoking in this building."

Because $50 per day was less than a room and meals at the hotel, I was pretty sure COMSAT would not quibble over the price.

He lit his third cigarette since we came in the place. "Still don't want to see it first?" Now he's playing the mind games with me.

I manage an embarrassed laugh. "Can I bring in our bags?"

"Might's well. I don't suppose you like ice cream." He turned his full attention to Lee.

Lee looked my way, proving this long trip had been worthwhile.

"Didn't ask him. Asked you," he addressed Lee again.

I nodded and Lee eagerly replied, "Sure do!"

"Only got vanilla. None of that fancy stuff. Still want it?"

"I like vanilla fine."

I left to get our bags from Karl's truck. "He actually gave you a room?" Karl was amazed. "You must have hit him on a good day."

"If that's a good day, I sure don't want to see a bad one," I laughed.

As we lugged the bags through the ringing door, Caroll began to poke more wood into the stove. "This way," a little old prune-faced woman stuck her head through the archway leading from the kitchen. "Don't bang the walls," she admonished as I struggled to follow her down a long, dimly lighted hallway with badly worn

36

linoleum reminiscent of the old kitchen in West Virginia. "And don't hit the furnace," she warned as we snaked past an old monster oil/wood combination furnace.

"I'll give you this room close to the bathroom for the boy. Hope he's a quiet one!" She opened the door to a very small room just large enough to hold two twin beds and a small dresser with a lamp on it. "You'll have to store those bags under the beds. I'll get you some hangers. There's a small closet next to the bath you can use for now, I suppose. Don't like to do that, but for a month…," she drifted away. I went to rescue Lee.

"Breakfast is at seven. Don't be late!" Caroll spit as we slunk off to our room.

Welcome to Talkeetna!

It would be nice to be able to say Crazy Karl, Evil Alice, and Caroll and Verna Close were the only strangeness encountered during our first two months in Talkeetna. Many of the other characters in Talkeetna would prove to make the above mentioned appear "normal" over the passage of time.

Crazy Karl latched onto me as if I were a long-lost brother. He was determined to be my personal guide and introduce me to everything and everybody in the area. For the most part this was not all bad. However, before the first month was over, I was becoming *overwhelmed!*

The Closes took a liking to Lee and pampered him to death, which was welcome, as I was very busy training technicians and monitoring the equipment installation at the earth station. Spending long late hours at work often caused me to miss the Roadhouse dinner time at six o'clock. Crazy Karl and I would usually eat together at Evil Alice's and have a drink or two, or more.

After the first two weeks Caroll allowed as how he might leave the side door unlocked after ten o'clock if I would lock it on my way in. "Don't come home drunk though," he admonished. "Don't allow drunks here," A sort of paradox, as the Roadhouse was the only liquor carry-out store in town.

Only two of the new technicians were transfers from other earth stations. None of the others had ever been close to satellite com-

munications. I enlisted the aid of the two transfers to help in training. The problem being, they were both about as screwy as Crazy
Karl. As a matter of fact, most of the new technicians were somewhat less than stable. I began to worry about my own sanity a
little. Was I as weird as the rest of these guys? Lord, I prayed not!

Merle Albert, one of the transfers, had several children in the
same age range as ours. His oldest son was the same age as Lee. His
wife and family were waiting to join him after school let out. Having this in common drew us into a friendship. He began to join
Karl and me at lunch and dinner. He had rented a cabin from a
woman named Mary Canary for $50 per month. He asked if Lee
and I might want to leave the Roadhouse and split the rent with
him. This would cut our monthly room and board from more than
$1,500 to $25 plus groceries, while COMSAT was still willing to
reimburse us at the $50 per day. "You bet!"

We left the Roadhouse and moved to the 16' x 20' cabin owned
by Mary Canary.

Possibly the most crazy of all the new site personnel proved to
be the Manager, William Punderson, and his more than slightly
promiscuous wife. I carefully avoided ever letting myself be caught
around her alone. I didn't need that!

The cabin, 1970.

My first big run-in with Punderson came with my first paycheck. At $240 per week, the check was more than one hundred dollars per week less than the $350 he had promised me in West Virginia. The $350 was barely enough to support a family of seven in Talkeetna, even in 1970. Never being bashful, I immediately brought this little oversight to his attention. To his knowledge, I had only been promised to be the highest paid technician at the site. No dollar value had been promised. I reminded him that both DeAnn and I had been present at the meeting in our home when he had promised me a $350-per-week salary. I also informed him that Crazy Karl was bragging that he was the highest paid technical person on the site at $246 per week.

My next paycheck was for $247 per week. From that day forward I worked exactly eight hours per day and forty hours per week. If requested to work any overtime, I forced the jerk to authorize it in writing ahead of time. I also contacted my old friend Williams, the COMSAT personnel manager, to let him know I was not happy.

"You can always come back to DC, Carl," was his response.

"Will you guys pay my expenses to move back?"

"I'll check it out, but I'm sure we won't. Besides that, we have already put your household goods on the barge. Sorry. If it is any consolation, you're not the only one claiming Punderson lied to them." This made me feel *much* better.

# CHAPTER 9

# My Trip From Hell

## (or How to Make Your Wife Appreciate Talkeetna)

*I, DeAnn, was to leave* the day after school let out and drive to Alaska with our four remaining children. Yes, I said drive. What the hell, Dave said, I was young and healthy. Why should he have all the grief?

It was *my* turn.

I swear no Chevy Chase movie could possibly hatch a plot to rival the problems we encountered on our drive to Alaska. Our car was a nearly new station wagon. To prepare for the trip, Dave's uncle had put four new six-ply Double Eagle tires on the car. My brother agreed to replace all the belts and hoses before the trip. There should be no problems. Piece of cake.

The first little mishap was when a picnic basket I had tied to the car-top carrier blew off while going along the Ohio turnpike. Fortunately, all the cars behind us managed to dodge the flying basket.

We pulled over, walked back, and picked up all the dishes we could find.

A few hours later as we were traveling through Chicago during rush hour, the car began to overheat. Steam was billowing from under the vehicle. By some miracle, all traffic stopped on the Chicago freeway during rush hour. We were able to limp off the freeway and find a service station. Thank God it was 1970 and still relatively safe to stop at a gas station in a large city. The thermostat had frozen closed, a common problem with cars in those days. A competent mechanic at the service station replaced the thermostat and we were on our merry way.

The next day we pulled into a service station in Wisconsin. The attendant—they had such things back then—informed me that my fan belt was badly worn. "It can't be," I smelled a scam. "My brother just replaced it!"

"Okay, fine," he slammed the hood down and came to the window to collect the money for the gas. This grandfather-aged man looked inside and saw this little young mother and all those bright eyed shiny faces traveling alone. His heart melted. "Look here, young lady, I just cannot allow you to go on without looking at this fan belt. Maybe your brother forgot to replace it. Please look."

He raised the hood while I, understandably suspicious and with our fourteen-year-old along for protection, moved cautiously around to look at the nearly destroyed fan belt. It seems my dear brother ran short of time and merely tossed the new fan belt in the back of the car without replacing it. With a new fan belt, the journey continued. By now all the kids and I were wondering what would be next! We didn't have to wait long.

Wanting to save money and time I decided to spend the night sacked out for a catnap at a roadside rest. There were several other cars in the parking area. Not wanting anyone to know I was a woman traveling alone with a bunch of children, I had our fourteen-year-old, Carl, escort the younger children to the restrooms and then told them to lock the car doors while I visited the same. All was progressing well until late in the night Carl decided to have an attack of claustrophobia. In a screaming fit, he rolled down the rear window and dove out onto the ground, forcing me to go out to calm him down. All the other kids jerked awake in terror. The inside of the car erupted into sheer bedlam. So much for the secrecy of being alone! Now wide awake, I decided to travel on, cursing Dave with every breath!

With only a week left to reach Prince Rupert and the ferry to Alaska, I decided to make some time on the interstate by driving my normal speed...*fast*. I began to feel an occasional strange shimmy in the steering wheel. I kept asking Carl if he felt it. He repeatedly assured me, "Mom, it's only your imagination."

My father being a mechanic, I knew enough about cars to feel certain something was not quite right. I pulled off the interstate and into a service station, asking the attendant to put the car on the rack and check out the tires. The attendant walked around the car and looked at all the tires. "I don't see anything wrong, lady."

I begged him to please put it up on the rack and check them anyway.

"Lady, if it will make you feel better, okay." Up went the car as the attendant circled to check each tire. "Oh my God!" he screamed as one of the rear tires fell off and bounced across the garage floor. He began to curse himself out for insisting we go back on the highway. Apparently, when Dave's uncle had installed the new tires, he had forgotten to tighten the lugs on that tire. God was once again looking out for us.

All these near disasters and we hadn't reached Canada yet. "What else could possibly go wrong?" I was lamenting. "Dave, *why Alaska?!*" He must have gypsy blood in his veins.

Finally reaching the Canadian border, I ran into an overly concerned border guard. He would not let me enter with the amount of cash I produced. "Are you certain you have no more?" he admonished.

"Okay, okay, do you have a restroom I can use?"

Using one of my mother's old tricks, I had more money in my bra. Stomping into the restroom, I ripped the money from my bra, stomped back, and showed it to the now satisfied and slightly embarrassed guard.

Another damn delay in getting at that gypsy!

The time schedule was growing shorter! I now had less than two days to reach the Prince Rupert ferry and more than 800 miles to go. I had no choice but to stop for only short naps and snacks for some very tired and moody kids. I was now cursing all his ancestors along with him!

What next?!

You ask, "What next?" and you get it! The road to Prince Rupert was undergoing major construction. Just for added interest, the

42

weather was rainy and the road was a sea of mud. It was too late to turn around and head back home to find a nasty divorce lawyer, so I slipped and slid over the muddy, rocky excuse for a road while praying I only lived long enough to get my hands around his scrawny neck. By some twist of fate we managed to reach Prince Rupert just in time to slide our lump of mud aboard the ferry to Alaska. At last, we were on the ferry. No more driving! I could remove the children and myself from the car and get some badly needed sleep!

However, when the gods decide to mess in your soup, they never do it halfway. Neither I nor any of the children had ever been on an oceangoing ferryboat before, let alone crammed into a lower inside berth. Our oldest daughter, Jeannie, and I were about to be introduced to a new kick in the ass called seasickness. We were both sick as dogs for the entire three-day voyage to Haines, Alaska. So much for finally being able to relax and get some badly needed sleep. I was now planning the gypsy's slow and agonizing death.

Painfully, coming to the end of a miserable voyage, our little band was deposited on the Haines dock. Horror of horrors, the Haines to Haines Junction highway was in even worse condition than the road to Prince Rupert! Ahead was one hundred miles of mud and rocks and then another six hundred miles on the ALCAN and Glenn highways to Talkeetna. The only two things keeping me going were the fact that I could tell myself in my mother's typical Russian style, "This too shall pass," and the anticipation that Dave would have to face me at the end of this journey.

After what seemed like an eternity, we finally exited the Haines "highway from hell" onto the ALCAN. We were treated to a relatively easy voyage along the ALCAN and Glenn superhighways, compared to the Prince Rupert and Haines.

My first impression of Alaska was, "Where are the trees?" Traveling along the highway in this section of south-central Alaska most trees are scrub spruce or stunted birch and aspen. Having just left a home in West Virginia surrounded by fifty-to-one-hundred-feet tall pine and cedar trees, these head-tall scrubs were quite a contrast.

Having reached the ALCAN early in the morning with only six hundred miles to go, after all the hell we had been through, we decided to push on nonstop to the end of this fiasco.

Reaching Palmer, Alaska, we only had about ninety miles to go. It was late afternoon. We stopped for a final potty, food, and fuel. How bad could the last ninety miles be? We might as well freshen up, eat, and have a nice leisurely final leg.

Remember, this was a new highway being pushed over what was previously a caterpillar tractor trailer ("cat trail" in common Alaskan slang) used by miners and trappers to Talkeetna. Also, recall how glad Dave was that Crazy Karl had picked him up in Anchorage with a 4WD truck. The new highway crossed half a dozen creeks and two rivers. Temporary construction-type bridges were installed across the rivers. No bridges across the creeks yet, just a relatively smooth path made by a cat. Ninety more miles of loose gravel road, delays at creek fording and *mud*. Was there to be no end?!

Small towns being what they are—and Talkeetna is typical—Forrest Englehorn, one of the locals, overheard this fiery little redhead talking about heading for Talkeetna to kill her husband while waiting her turn at a creek ford. He rushed up the highway in his 4WD truck to inform the whole town and Dave that trouble was on the way. As Crazy Karl and Dave were preparing to jump in his truck and head down the highway to meet me, guess who pulled up in front of her new 16' x 20' tar-paper shack home? The car stopped and the engine went silent. No activity. Our son Carl put into words exactly what I was thinking. "Mom, if someone paid me a million dollars I would not make this trip again!"

Karl and Dave cautiously approached the mud-caked vehicle. Opening the door they were greeted by what can only be described as five silent, large eyed owls.

"So, this is *home?*" I weakly managed. "Where's the bed?" I fell into Dave's arms as pale and thin as I have ever been.

"Why Alaska?" I whispered as he half-carried me to the door.

# CHAPTER 10

# DeAnn Describes Her First Summer in Alaska

## (or There Really Is a Hell on Earth!)

*My first day in Talkeetna* after Carl, Jeannie, D'Aun, Patrick, and I arrived in the late afternoon. I still don't remember how I knew exactly where the cabin was. I think the shock of seeing the 16' x 20' tar-paper shingled cabin wiped out that memory. I do remember the two 55-gallon drums of oil that were sitting near the front door. I later learned these drums of oil were used to fire the noisy, smelly old stove that resembled an old-fashioned wood cookstove. This was also our hot water and heat. At least there was *hot* running water and a real bathroom with a toilet. One of the conditions for my agreement to come to Alaska had been to have running water.

Dave had promised me there would be running water. I later heard him tell Carl and Lee they would build the cabin over a stream and the water could run in one end and out the other. I had quickly informed him that was not acceptable. So, after half carrying my exhausted body into the cabin he eagerly turned on the kitchen faucet to immediately show me the "running water."

"Bathroom?" I dared ask. He flung open the door to the small bathroom and flushed the toilet.

The first week in Talkeetna is one I will *never* forget. The initial shock and introduction to our living quarters was somewhat softened the following weekend when we attended the local school graduation ceremony. Keith Miller, Governor of Alaska, was the commencement speaker. Later in the evening we had the pleasure of talking with him over at the Talkeetna Teepee Bar, "Evil Alice's," as it was usually called. The odds of an occurrence like this happening back in our home state of Ohio were pretty slim.

The location of our cabin put us in the proximity of most of the activity in this "quaint" village. When we heard gunshots a couple nights later it made my hair stand on end. The proprietor of a local bar had shot her husband. Apparently, a women patron had become *too* friendly and the husband had not rejected the attention. An argument ensued and the wife pulled out a .45 from under the bar and shot him as he ran from the building. She blew one shoulder nearly off, but didn't kill him. He refused to press charges saying, "I deserved it." Where had I moved to?!

The next day one of the construction workers from the site had a temper tantrum, taking an axe to the nonworking pay telephone booth that stood outside the Fairview Inn.

A few days later there was another scary incident at the Roadhouse. Caroll Close always served a family-style dinner in the evening, which Dave and I decided to join. The clientele all sat at a long table and after the main meal Caroll would ask what everyone wanted for dessert, even though he had only one type of dessert and that was what everyone was going to get. He had been serving strawberries and ice cream every night. When he asked for the dessert preferences, one of the construction workers asked for pie, but of course was given the strawberries and ice cream, which he proceeded to pitch right through the window. Now I knew everyone here was crazy!

We lived very close to the village airstrip. This strip was used mostly by the locals, such as Don Sheldon and Cliff Hudson. One evening both of these pilots were coming in for a landing. I don't actually remember which one refused to give way to the other but tempers flared when they finally landed. One of the pilots took a hammer to the other's plane wing. In retaliation, the other sawed off his rival's tail section with a chain saw!

My first encounter with a *big* wild animal…the moose! One afternoon Merle's wife, Roseanne Albert, and her four children were over visiting. We were all in the cabin having lunch when we suddenly heard this horrible pounding and kicking on the side of the cabin. We looked out to see a large moose using her back hoofs to kick with all her might at the side of the building. She actually put big holes in the cabin with her hooves. I don't know what set of eyes in that cabin were the largest, but I am sure mine matched them. We later found that the reason the mama moose was so unhappy was because she had just had twin calves in the woods behind the cabin and our son Lee and his friend Jay had found one of the calves. It was dead. Being young boys they had to investigate a little closer and touch it. Apparently, the mama moose followed their scent back to our cabin and she was going to get them for hurting her baby.

As if all these crazy incidents were not enough, we had our first earthquake. Another one of my wrong impressions was that during *any* earthquake the ground always opened wide and you dropped into a big hole. Well, guess where I was when this first earthquake hit? Ya…on the toilet with my pants around my ankles! As the cabin rocked and rolled all I could see was this picture of myself sitting on a toilet with my pants around my ankles at the bottom of a large hole.

Later that fall we had another good-sized earthquake that had a funny story to go with it. Dave had bought a couple of used Polaris snow machines and he was working on one of the engines in a little out building behind the cabin, and things were not going well. He came into the cabin swearing, vowing he was going to blow up the so-and-so if it didn't start. A few minutes later the cabin shook so hard it was like an explosion and I thought he had actually blown up the engine—but it was *only* a big earthquake.

You have to understand that before Dave came home in 1969 and announced, "Guess where we are moving to next spring?" I had never given Alaska a thought. The only impressions of Alaska I had were ones of snow, bears, igloos, and Eskimos. I was not prepared for this place I would much later in life come to love and call home. The mountains were majestic but the vegetation was a disappointing surprise. The trees looked scrawny and sickly compared to the large oak and maple trees I had been raised with and loved. I thought all "towns" had houses with lawns. You can imagine my shock when I arrived in Talkeetna to see not only no lawns, or large tree-lined streets, but old dilapidated cars lining the main street. The "streets" were mostly dirt and mud with a little gravel thrown in. The buildings, for the most part, needed paint and repairs.

Thinking I could be helpful I approached one of the town "matriarchs" and suggested we should get a group together and remove all the old cars from main street. I was told it wasn't necessary because in the winter they were covered with snow and in summer everyone was too busy fishing to care. Many years later a friend of mine did get some of this town cleanup accomplished, but it was after I left town.

Some of my least endearing memories of that first summer will always be the fishing trips and picking blueberries in the snow.

I did not, and still don't, enjoy fishing. Dave generally insisted that most fishing trips be family outings to remote streams only accessible by a long drive and another long hike through bear- and moose-infested "jungle." I now realize, later in life, that he really was attempting to do something he hoped the whole family would enjoy together. Nevertheless, the girls and I generally begged off the long hikes and remained in the truck to read a book. He and the boys would return hours later, dirty, smelly, tired, and cranky. They would always be dragging several fish, which had to be washed in the bathtub and then cleaned on my kitchen counter. Yuck!

One of the more enjoyable fishing trips took place in late June of 1970. We piled all the kids in the pickup and drove about seventy miles up the new Parks Highway, under construction between Talkeetna and Fairbanks. We stopped and parked on the south side of the Chulitna River. Only a footbridge used by the construction workers was installed at the time. The guys all grabbed backpacks and fishing poles and each held a whining girl's hand as we snaked across the swinging footbridge. *Some fun this was!*

Reaching the other side, we approached a small cabin belonging to Mary Canary. Dave informed me this was her "homestead" and we were welcome to stay overnight in the cabin. There was a path out back to…the woods, *not* the outhouse. Even an outhouse would have been a welcome sight to me! The girls and I grabbed toilet paper and headed sheepishly down the "path," absolutely certain the biggest bear in the world was waiting for us around every corner.

Everyone…refreshed…the boys informed us the fishing stream was a three-mile hike to a creek named "Troublesome." Sounded like a perfect name to me! An hour later we broke out of the tangled alder and willow lining the creek path to a sandbar along the Chulitna River. Before us was the most breathtaking view I have ever seen. The entire Alaskan Range, dominated by Mount McKinley, rose majestically behind the river.

While the girls and I collapsed on a patch of sandy beach, the boys began assembling fishing gear. Dave's native friends had told him the mouth of this creek was one of the best grayling and trout streams in the world. You might also snag into a "king or two" they informed him. He had neglected to ask just what a "king" was.

It was already late afternoon and everyone was getting a little hungry. "Oh, no," one of the boys exclaimed. "We left the back-pack with the food in the cabin!"

Just then, one of the boys got a huge fish on his line. Among all of them they managed to get it to the shore. It was about a thirty-pound salmon! "This must be what they call a king," Dave announced excitedly.

"I'd rather call it dinner!" I was noticeably agitated.

"Okay, maybe we can." Dave instructed the boys to build a campfire inside a pile of rocks while he emptied out his metal tackle box. He cut a large filet from the fish, laid it in the tackle box, and set it on some of the rocks after the fire had turned to red coals.

We passed the tackle box around on a piece of driftwood and all took turns eating the salmon with Dave's hunting knife. It was the most delicious thing any of us had ever eaten.

While the rest of the family was licking the tackle box clean, Dave began running up and down the bank of the river with a fishing pole bent almost double in his hands. A *huge* fish suddenly jumped from the water shaking its head and tail. This happened several times. Each time the fish would jump, it would change direction, first upstream, then downstream. After what seemed an eternity, the fish swam right in front of us and rolled on its back.

"Grab the damn thing!" Dave shouted to the boys. Dutifully, Carl and Lee both jumped into the water up to their waist, grabbed the fish, and threw it on the bank. It was a fifty-five-pound king salmon! We stayed until each of the boys had caught a salmon of their own. They then cut an alder branch about ten feet long and strung the cleaned fish through the gill openings on the poll. Carl and Dave were to carry those fish the long three miles out of there. The rest of us were now loaded down with the backpacks.

**Big Fishing Trip.**

About halfway back to the cabin, our little seven-year-old daughter D'Aun looked up at her father and made the most touching plea I have ever heard. "Daddy, my legs won't come up anymore." Dave gently reached down, picked her up, and placed her on the shoulder opposite from the fish litter. Carl then reached down and did the same for little five-year-old Patrick.

About a half hour later we all fell exhausted in sleeping bags scattered around the floor of the little cabin. I looked at my watch. It was 3:00 AM. With the long daylight hours none of us had realized how awfully late it was. What a wonderful day!

Not having much money that year, we did a lot of fishing for food. Dave and his new friend Hans Donoho shot a moose and a bear, which we shared. We picked every wild berry growing in the valley. I made jelly from raspberries, wild strawberries, cranberries, and anything else that appeared to be edible.

Having heard that blueberries were exceptionally nutritious, we decided to head up the highway on Labor Day to pick blueber-

50

ries. About the time we found a field covered with beautiful berries, it began to snow! Every one of us had a large fruit juice can that Dave gave instructions to fill before we would leave for home. It was snowing so hard we had to brush the snow away to find the berries. Poor little Jeannie, D'Aun, Patrick, and I had almost frozen hands before we finally rebelled! Even Carl and Lee who would normally, without question, follow Dave into hell, finally had it!

"That's it, Dad," they chorused. "If you want any more of these things, *do it yourself!* We are going back to the truck and get some heat!"

Dave began to laugh at his own idiocy. "This is a little dumb, isn't it?" he sighed.

We all trudged back through the snow with *enough* blueberries to suit us all.

The end of the summer found me enrolling the kids in school. While doing this the school principal asked me if I would be willing to fill out an application for substitute teaching. I told him I didn't have a teaching degree but he as-

Another fishing trip.

sured me it wasn't necessary in the remote areas. I reluctantly filled out the application after he reassured me I probably wouldn't be called on very often to fill in as a substitute teacher.

So much for that promise. The night before school started we came home to a note attached to our cabin door that said, "Don't Panic but be at school tomorrow morning." Another new experience, one that I truly enjoyed. I filled in for the high school science and math teacher, who had resigned, for six weeks while the district searched for a permanent replacement. Dave and I were doing chemistry experiments at home the night before so I could explain them in class. After the six weeks in the high school classroom, I filled in for the first and second grade for a couple of weeks. In fact, I ended up working almost every day for that complete school year. I loved being around the kids and really enjoyed the years I spent in the school system. I went on to work as the school secretary for several more years.

CHAPTER 11

# Dave's Turn to Continue This Saga

## (or Alaska Does Not Prove to Be My Paradise)

*The months of June* and July in 1970 were some of the rainiest in the history of Talkeetna. It rained every day, which caused havoc with the site construction. The weather, coupled with my ongoing feud with Punderson, did not help my disposition. Every day I regretted more and more my decision to leave the calm and gentle life of West Virginia.

August ushered in my second big run-in with Punderson. The company housing compound where all COMSAT employees and their families were expected to live and pay rent of $500 per month plus utilities was, in my view, a disaster. The electric rate in Talkeetna was a horrible twelve cents per kilowatt-hour. This rate was five to six times the national average. The "compound" homes were to be heated with propane gas, hauled 120 miles from Anchorage, which made it even more expensive than the electric. As if the high electric and propane bills were not bad enough, the "homes" were, in fact, California-style double-wide house trailers with hardly any insulation, placed on uninsulated concrete block daylight basements. Talkeetna is in an exceptionally cold area. Winter temperatures often reach thirty to forty degrees *below* zero for long periods of time.

Calling on my past knowledge from my building background in a cold climate, I presented to Punderson a list of minimal upgrades required to make these dogs livable. He informed me that he held a degree in civil engineering and therefore felt he was more qualified than I to judge the fitness of the structures. He tore up my list in front of me.

"At the cost of propane and electricity coupled with your outrageous rent payment, your technicians will be spending all of their paychecks just to keep a roof over their heads. Are you crazy?" I shouted. "Count me out! I will never live in one of your crummy California house trailers."

"You will or find another job!" he screamed.

"There are at least three of the new hires living outside your compound, mister. If you fire me, you had better fire them. I signed no contract stating I would live in your compound just as you signed no contract promising me a living wage to stay in this hellhole! Do you really want to push this?"

"G-g-get out of my office and do your job," he stammered. "You'll never find a place to live around here. Remember that I was in your home in West Virginia. Your wife will never allow herself to live in a Talkeetna shack. You'll be begging me to move into one of the company houses before winter is over."

This was not entirely a rash prediction on his part. But he obviously did not know DeAnn or how prone I was to bullying her into anything I believed was necessary. He also was not aware that I had already arranged to rent the 16' x 20' tar-paper cabin owned by "sweet old" Mary Canary. Remembering DeAnn's prediction that we would be living in a one-room tar-paper shack with no running water, I was not about to share this bit of good news with her until the shock of her trip from hell had subsided. Also, I was scared to death to tell her!

One evening several weeks after her arrival, over several drinks at the Teepee with our new friends Hans and Jackie Donoho, I managed to, with their help, explain to DeAnn the folly of entering the compound. I promised DeAnn this was only temporary. We would improve our living conditions, but not just yet. In the spring. Not being completely convinced, she reluctantly agreed. Whew!

Punderson was amazed. This showed how little he knew about my loving confidant.

We finally managed to get the earth station on the air in the first week of July. The grand opening dedication ceremony was attended by the president and vice president of COMSAT. Also in attendance were the wife of the former senator Bartlett and the very first Alaskan governor, William Egan, and Mrs. Egan. Punderson was so busy trying to impress the COMSAT big shots that he had to reluctantly turn the Egans over to me to serve as their tour guide. They proved to be a very gracious and enjoyable couple.

A grand dedication ball was planned that evening at Evil Alice's. A valid reason for DeAnn to dress up and enjoy something formal in Alaska. She magically became her old poised, relaxed, and absolutely gorgeous self once again. For this evening she was again in her element, not a slave to my wannabe backwoodsman fantasies.

After dinner and early evening conversation with the governor and the Closes at the Roadhouse, we decided to join the ball at Evil Alice's Teepee. The party was in full swing when we arrived. Karl Whelm immediately descended upon us to inform me that Punderson's wife was presently entwined in the arms of the site construction manager beneath the pool table. After failing to extricate her, an embarrassed Punderson left in a huff.

"Isn't that a crying shame?" Karl did a little dance of glee as he drifted around the room and under the pool table snapping pictures. "Let the party begin. We may need these later for blackmail, my friend," he sang with an evil glint in his eye, pointing to his camera.

A few days after the dedication, a Sunday, the new Talkeetna Earth Station went off the air due to a hard earthquake that shook our little old cabin nearly off its foundation. The shake was followed shortly by a call from Punderson, ordering me to the site. Upon arrival I found the duty technician cowering outside the building and refusing to reenter. When the quake hit, he had been in the elevator ascending to the upper level. The elevator cable jumped off the reel and the compartment fell about fifteen feet. He had climbed out, shaken out his shorts, and promptly exited the building. "You want it fixed, you do it. I ain't going back in there. I quit!" He was still shaking.

"Calm down, will you? It was only an earthquake, for crying out loud," I put an arm around his shoulders. By now, several other technicians and Punderson had arrived and were circling the entrance.

The frightened duty technician and I explained the situation to Punderson. While Punderson attempted to calm the duty technician, two other techs and I entered to check the system status. It took almost a week to repair all the damaged equipment and get back on the satellite. New earthquake mounts and bracing were added to all primary system equipment.

The rain continued unabated through July and August. The only thing DeAnn hates more than hot weather is rainy weather. The rain and mud, coupled with the nearly impossible task of comfortably stuffing a family of seven into the small one-room cabin, raised tensions to a fever pitch.

In preparations for the coming winter, we insulated a portion of the small attic just large enough for the two older boys to sleep in. We converted the small pantry to a quasi bedroom for the girls. The youngest slept on an air mattress under the table. De and I occupied a sagging single bed in one corner of the cabin.

When our furniture and all our other possessions arrived, it created another problem. Where were we to put all this stuff? There was no mini-storage in Talkeetna. There was a rickety old wood-shed behind the cabin into which we stuffed a van-load of valuable possessions, except for the piano, two loveseats, our dining room table, and our king-sized bed. The one-room cabin was now wall-to-wall bed, piano, table, oil fired combination heating stove, refrigerator, and kitchen sink. The boys and I hurriedly re-roofed the woodshed between raindrops!

By late August the rain had subsided somewhat but the mornings were already frosty.

While enrolling the children for the following year and sign-

Inside Talkeetna cabin,
winter—1970–71.

ing herself up as a substitute teacher, DeAnn met one of the teachers and began explaining our "cozy little cabin" arrangement to him. He told her he had an old camper trailer out behind his place that he would be willing to lend us for some added storage space. He would also help haul it to us if we could find a truck with a trailer hitch. The new school secretary, Jackie Donoho, overheard the conversation and volunteered her husband Hans along with his truck. The next morning Hans and I dragged the old 8' x 12' trailer to the cabin and located it so that the trailer entrance door was directly behind the rear door of the cabin. We spent the following day installing a small hallway between the two doors. We built a platform in the front of the trailer and installed our king-sized bed on it. We now had a private bedroom and I had a new friend. Things were looking up!

Winter fun in Talkeetna.

CHAPTER 12

# Attempting to Make the Best of an Impossible Situation

*Trying to settle in* and make a new life in Talkeetna was not easy.

DeAnn was now kept very busy as "substituting" turned to a full-time job when one of the teachers decided to resign.

On the heels of a fall of working late and partying hard, November came in as a heavy blanket of cold. The frost crept into the little cabin and turned everything not within ten feet of the small drip-pot oil cooking and heating stove to ice. Whenever anyone opened the entry door, a huge wave of frigid air would be sucked from outside and roll across the floor toward the stove fan. Several times, the stove quit from ice in the unfiltered line. A daily battle just to keep the stove operating ensued.

A copper coil wound through the stove's drip-pot burner. This coil fed our hot water tank. A very ingenious little system unless the copper water coil decided to rupture.

The entire family was attending some evening school function. Upon returning to the cabin I was the first to open the door. DeAnn and the girls were still in the car. The first indication that something was wrong was the smell. Next was the site of nothing but black inside the cabin. I closed the door and told Carl to inform his mother that she was to take the three youngest children and go visit Hans and Jackie. They were to stay there until I called and told her to come home.

What to do? and Where to begin? were the big questions. It

was thirty below zero, our fire was out and there was an inch of black, oily soot blanketing the entire interior of the cabin. Lord, but I was now truly hating this place!

We had a large commercial vacuum cleaner in the woodshed. The boys and I plugged it into the closest outlet to the front door. We carefully and painstakingly began to suck up the black gunk ahead of us as we moved through the cabin. The boys continued to vacuum while I turned off the water pump and inspected for water damage. When the pipe ruptured, the water pump had come on, flooding the fire pot, and then continued to overflow and flood the cabin floor with black greasy slim. Most of the water was exiting through the crack around a trap door leading to the crawl space beneath the cabin. The mess in the crawl area would have to wait for another day. While the boys mopped in the now very cold cabin, I shut off the valve into and out of the hot water system and cut the lines so as to remove the drip-pot copper coil. We all then began to sponge water from the drip pot. Hours later, with frost in our nostrils and our fingers and toes nearly frozen, we managed to have most of the soot cleaned, the floor mopped dry, and a flicker of flame in the oil drip pot. Lord, was I proud of these boys. They had sensed the urgency of the situation and responded accordingly. No complaints, no bickering, no whining. What great sons!

Another hour, and the cabin was nearly livable, except for the heavy oil smell. We sprayed tons of Lysol all over the place, called DeAnn, and told her to come on home. I left the boys with the chore of describing the evening's events to her as I just didn't have the courage. We let all the children crowd into our little bedroom out back for the next few days as the sickening combination of oil and air freshener in the main cabin was impossible to breathe.

The following week my aunt phoned me at the earth station. My father had been killed in an automobile accident.

Life can be so unfair at times. My father had been upset beyond description when I decided to move to Alaska. He screamed in my face that he would never speak to me again. He never did.

The multitude of disappointments attached to the move to Alaska had already begun to take its toll on us personally and on our marriage. Now another straw was being added to the camel's back. My mother was a basket case. My brother James, now also in Alaska, had no money for a plane ticket to Ohio. DeAnn and I were not exactly flush either. Who could take care of our children while we returned to Ohio?

I would later suggest to DeAnn that we sell everything in Alaska and all go home to the farm. For reasons I never really understood, nor had the time or desire to ponder, she absolutely refused.

Hans came to our rescue. He insisted they could take care of our five children along with their own five for the two weeks Punderson would allow me to be away. Our banker graciously allowed us to write a rubber check to buy airline tickets for DeAnn, my brother, and myself.

My thoughts during the long plane trip to Ohio were unbelievably morose. Suicide seemed a plausible solution. How I despised my life! DeAnn was in an even worse state of mind. For the first time in our lives we did not take the time to confide in each other or share in each other's pain. An invitation to disaster.

My father's funeral, helping my mother through probate, and all the other little nagging details requiring attention only deepened my despair. My mother was in no condition to be left alone. DeAnn would not move back to Ohio. Punderson insisted I return to Alaska or lose my job. My children were still in Alaska. Damn it *all!* After all these years, had God forsaken my marriage and me?

The temporary solution was to have my mother return to Alaska with us. We now had mom, my brother and his live-in, our five kids, and two puppies they had inherited during our absence. The little cabin was stuffed to overflowing. Mom had to sleep with DeAnn and me in our king-sized bed. The little military oil stove could not keep the cold weather outside. The three of us breathing heavily in our sleep released so much moisture in the air that the bedcovers

De and Mom on pipeline—1978.

would be frozen to the outer walls every morning. Bathroom logistics alone were mind-boggling. Thank goodness the rear of the cabin backed up to the great wilderness. But it was forty degrees below zero!

All being rather low on money, Hans, Jackie, DeAnn, and I took our 1968 station wagon that DeAnn and the kids had driven to Alaska into Anchorage and sold it at a used car lot. We spent the night together in a room at the old Northern Lights Hotel getting drunk and playing card games. The next day we shopped all over town for Christmas presents. Stuffing all four of us into the Donoho pickup, the presents all in the pickup bed, we headed back to Talkeetna.

Christmas Eve the boys and I took our pickup and hunted along the road for a small spruce tree, which we jammed into one corner of the cabin. DeAnn and Mom wrapped presents and piled them under the little tree. Although none of us was really in much of a celebration mood, we managed to put on a "sort of" Christmas spirit for the sake of each other.

December was coming to an end and no break in the cold weather was evident. DeAnn agreed to accompany Mom back to Ohio. I half jokingly told Carl and Lee they had better kiss their mother good-bye and hold her tight, as this was probably the last time we'd ever see her.

New Year's Eve 1971 I spent feeling sorry for myself and getting drunk with Hans and some other friends. De called me at home at midnight in Ohio, and I was out partying. I called her at midnight my time, four in the morning in Ohio, and she was *not* happy. Happy New Year, my ass!

De stayed with my Mom for another week. Upon returning, she found my brother had rented another old cabin in town and I had banished the growing puppies to a corner of the woodshed. Life was a *little* less complicated.

We both agreed that another winter in Talkeetna like this one was definitely out of the question. We approached Mary Canary to ask if she would consider selling the cabin and the one acre lot it sat on to us. She eagerly agreed to sell for $5,000. We were to pay her $2,500 up front and she would hold a land contract for the balance. Using everything we owned as collateral, including the as yet unsold Ohio lakefront property, we approached the bank in Palmer to obtain an owner-builder construction loan. We planned to add a two-story 24' x 32' "addition" to the cabin. The loan committee, under advice of the bank president, was going to turn us down because he felt we "needed more experience building in Alaska." A darling woman loan officer by the name of Zane Jones came to our rescue by reminding them northern Ohio climate was not that different from south-central Alaska. "He has *lots* of experience there," Zane insisted. She swayed the loan committee enough to get us about half the amount we were asking for, probably saving our marriage.

With the slimmed-down building budget, much innovation was called for. In early April, my brother James and I had DeAnn drive us to Anchorage where we rented the largest flatbed truck Hertz could provide. We loaded the truck with a huge pile of dunnage (slang for lumberyard pallet and crating material) stacked behind the United Lumber Supply office. We paid a hundred dollars for enough material to frame the lower level and most of the second story of our new "mansion." The catch was that we had to take the entire pile or no deal. As we were creeping out of Anchorage with a load so heavy the tail of our rental truck was nearly dragging on the pavement, we noticed the state weigh scale light was flashing yellow, indicating all trucks must stop for weighing check. "Dammit, I hate this place!" I screamed.

It had begun to snow heavily, forcing traffic to slow to a crawl. The nearly blinding snowstorm hatched a plot in our giddy minds. If we could manage to get over into the oncoming lane just long enough to keep a line of traffic between us and the scale house, maybe we could sneak past them unobserved. If they caught us, we could play dumb and claim we thought only tractor trailer rigs were required to stop. We got lucky, forcing only one car off into the berm. It worked! But, just in case we had *not* pulled the "crime of the century" undetected, we immediately pulled off the main highway and hid behind the North Slope restaurant in Eagle River. It was *really* snowing now, and we still had 130 grueling miles to go. We decided to get a hamburger at the North Slope, pick up a bottle of bourbon fortification, and head north. Sometime after midnight we miraculously managed to limp into Talkeetna filled with a juvenile joy provided by a combination of the bourbon and our ability to avoid the law. I informed the boys they had to unload the truck immediately as we had to return it the next morning. Thank God for those sons, once again.

Anticipating an early spring, in May the boys and I began to punch holes in the still frozen ground to pour pillars supporting our new home. DeAnn's parents arrived in June ready to help. Over the next two months, the combined efforts of DeAnn's father, my brother, and my overworked and underpaid sons enabled us to frame and rough in the soon to be largest home in Talkeetna. The nastiest part of the job fell to Carl, Lee, and our youngest son, Patrick, who was now six. The dunnage was filled with bent nails that needed to be removed. All, to this day, never tire of reminding me about that thankless chore!

In July, James left for Ohio to help Mom sell the last remaining farm. From there he headed to Monterey, California, to open an art gallery, hoping to make a living selling some of the many watercolor paintings he had done in Ohio and Alaska.

In August, Mom called and offered to use some of Dad's insurance money to pay for our flight to Monterey so all of us could have a little family reunion. Punderson reluctantly agreed to give me another two-week vacation. We left the kids in the care of DeAnn's parents and took the triangle flight through Honolulu to Los Angeles. We rented a car in LA and drove the coast to Monterey. This trip helped start the healing process caused by all the turmoil of the past year. While we were on our trip, DeAnn's father finished wiring and plumbing our new home.

For the next three months I spent as little time as possible at the site. Evenings and weekends Hans and I generally disappeared into the woods to fish, hunt, and drink.

When problems come, they never come alone. On the trip back to Ohio, DeAnn's parents were in an auto accident that threw her dad's head into the car windshield. He never fully recovered, unexpectedly passing away in November. I was not up to facing Punderson, so I called his secretary and asked her to tell him we would be begging the airlines for an emergency seat to go to another funeral.

# CHAPTER 13

# Either This Guy Goes or *We Do!*

*Returning to Alaska,* we found the stressful situations resuming relentlessly. This was not only true for us, but everyone under Punderson's control. Someone at company headquarters must have taken notice that not only our marriage but several others in the group were beginning to unravel. The very first words from Punderson's mouth upon my return from my father-in-law's funeral were, "It is time to put your perceived problems behind you and get back to work!"

This uncalled-for remark had been made in the presence of several other site personnel, all of whom flinched noticeably at his lack of discretion.

For months now, I had been making plans to get out from under this clod. Crazy Karl, having been one of the witnesses to Punderson's insulting remark, approached me later that day with a plan. While we were at the funeral in Ohio, he had approached an Anchorage union business agent and asked the guy about the possibility of unionizing our shop. "Will you go with me to talk to him?"

"I'll have to think about that one, Karl. When is this meeting to take place?"

"The sooner the better." He then began to fill me in on all the problems Punderson had been creating for the other site personnel. It became apparent Punderson's rotten tricks were not directed only at me.

"Okay, tell the union guy we'll meet with him. I guess it can't hurt." I was still very skeptical of this approach, but figured the guy wouldn't show anyway.

To my surprise and dread, a week later the business agent called and asked us to meet with him at the Teepee bar. He suggested the union probably would not be interested in our small group. He did suggest we might "accidentally" scatter some union literature around the site where Punderson couldn't help but find it. That we did.

I don't know exactly what Karl and I had expected from Punderson, but he certainly reacted! A few days after scattering some union applications around the site, Karl and I were ushered into his office. He informed his second in command, a nice alcoholic guy named Doug Cloud, to keep everyone away from the door as he closed it. "I know you two sons of bitches are behind this!" He threw several of the union applications on the floor. Some had been filled out by site technicians. "I know this is designed to make me look bad in DC. If there is any more of this you are both fired!" He was now shaking uncontrollably. "There will be no damn union here. None of the COMSAT sites are unionized and this will not be the first one. That will go on my record over my dead body."

"If that's what it takes," Karl pushed it. That did it.

"Get the hell out of here!" The veins in his neck nearly exploded. "You're both fired!"

"You fire us and I'll be on the phone to DC within the hour. Is that what you want?" Karl was unrelenting.

"I-I-I'll make your lives so d-d-damn miserable you'll *all* quit! Get out of my office!"

The result of our little threat proved to be just the opposite of what we had intended. *No* trick was now too dirty for Punderson. Until now the rent and utilities had been paid locally by the "compound" inhabitants. Several of the technicians were behind on payments. Somehow, Punderson now talked payroll in DC into directly deducting these arrears. Two or three of the more solvent technicians found themselves lending money to the less solvent just to keep them in food. The local grocer in Talkeetna was allowing sizable credit accounts to build up. Karl and I suddenly became *extremely unpopular* with most of the other site personnel, much to Punderson's delight.

"Let's kill the bastard!" was Crazy Karl's solution. It was something to consider.…

"Maybe we can reason with him as a group," I foolishly suggested.

"Would you be willing to present our grievances?" he immediately responded.

"Why do I get the impression you're setting me up…again?"

"Who?…Me?…Would I do that to my best friend?" He feigned disbelief.

"Yes, you sure as hell would!"

"Okay, okay. You got me. Because we got all the other guys into such deep shit with Punderson, they have asked us to make a last-ditch effort to bring the asshole to reality. They want one of us to present the following list of 'requests' to him." Karl handed me a scratched-down list of ten complaints.

"These look a little more like demands than requests. Are these *everyone's* demands or merely yours?"

"I swear it is a consensus of the group. Would I lie?"

"Yes, you would. I assume by '*us*' presenting this, you really mean *me*, you chicken shit." I jabbed at him as I finished reading the list.

"You're so much more diplomatic than I," he weaseled.

"Yeah, sure."

Being far out on a limb was nothing new in my life, but never before had I heard the sound of the saw cutting off that limb so loud as at my reading of the "consensus" list to Punderson at a meeting held in his home. Most demands addressed problems in the "compound" and really had nothing to do with me. But, I foolishly pushed on:

I.  Insulated basements were required. Would the company buy insulation?

II. Woodstoves would greatly reduce the heating bills. Would the company buy them if the renters did the installation?

III. The average rent for any home in Talkeetna was $200 per month. Why was the company charging $400?

IV. What had brought about the automatic payroll deduction for rent?

V. Why were we forced to do the MAD, where all technicians rotated weekly from midnights to afternoons to days, rather than bidding single shifts for a year or more at a time? (Though I did not work this rotation, this one, I agreed with. A stupid requirement!)

The deeper I got into the list of demands, the more and more alone I began to feel in the crowd.

"Does anyone else share Carl's feelings here?" Punderson quizzed.

No response was forthcoming. Killing Crazy Karl immediately came to my mind. Now what do I do? Help me, God!

"I'm so sorry, Mr. Punderson. I guess this was only my own personal observation. Sorry to have taken up your time." I glared at Crazy Karl as DeAnn and I slunk from the place.

"I hate my life!" I screamed as we headed home in our pickup. DeAnn kept silent.

Through the rest of the winter I did only what was absolutely necessary at the site. I trained no more technicians. If they asked a question, I handed them the equipment manual and said, "Read!" I told Karl Whelm to stay the hell out of my face, forever.

Most of the winter, De and I spent cross-country skiing, snow machining, and partying with Hans and other friends not associated with the site. The paranoid Punderson was now certain *everyone* in Talkeetna was out to get him. He was probably not far from wrong. He retaliated by docking pay for each and every little infringement such as fifteen-minutes-late arrival on shifts.

Technicians with children in school functions were now prohibited from shift switching with bachelor guys so as to attend school functions.

More and more…more and more.

66

My own selfish feelings were only that they *deserved* it all. The gutless bastards! It didn't bother me one way or another, because as third in command, and the only one qualified to handle the daily live TV news and sports feeds from New York and LA to Anchorage, I did not work the MAD shift. And I was now not about to train anybody else to do my job!

Our second spring in Alaska finally arrived, and with it, a certified letter to second in command, Doug Cloud. The letter contained an official petition to be signed by any site personnel requesting the removal of William Punderson as site manager of the Talkeetna Earth Station. Cloud posted the petition on the canteen bulletin board. The next day it disappeared. Cloud posted it again. Within three days everyone at the site but one had signed. The one being me. Remembering how devastated I had been by the petition my AT&T technicians had circulated trying to remove me from my first supervisor position, I just couldn't do that to another human being. Not even Punderson.

I might as well have signed it though. The dumb SOB blamed me for the petition! He hauled me into his office and, with tears in his eyes, blamed me for destroying his career.

"Bill," I pled. "I had *nothing* to do with this. I didn't even sign it."

"That's further proof you are behind it!"

"Huh? How did you come to that conclusion?"

"You're after my job. I'll never leave here! I'll make your life miserable!" he ranted.

"I wouldn't have your job on a silver platter. You deserve it." I numbly responded. What a jerk!

I called my old buddy Jack Williams in COMSAT personnel and told him I needed a three-month leave of absence or I would go insane. He said no problem, consider it effective the day he received my request in writing. I priority mailed it that day. There were no fax machines yet.

Punderson had won this round.

# CHAPTER 14

# Stress

*Some headquarters wag* put the following stress chart, I think copied from the *Reader's Digest,* in the monthly company newsletter. According to the chart's attached directions, each stress factor in a couple's life was given a weighting factor. On this chart, the author estimated the "nervous breakdown" point to be somewhere around stress factors adding up to 100 during a one-year period. According to the article, the following were the major stress factors and associated weighting:

- Change of Job: 10
- Moving Family: 10
- Death in the Family: 30
- Trouble on the Job: 10
- Extramarital Problems: 30
- Monetary Problems: 30

Over the past year every one of the stress factors on this list, to one degree or another, had been eroding our marriage and the lives of most of the other people enslaved by Punderson and COMSAT. The result being a band of very unhappy souls.

In our own case:

- We obviously changed jobs: 10
- We moved the family: 10
- Both of our fathers died: 60
- My new boss hated me: 10
- Lack of money due to pay cut: 30
- There were some *extraordinary* marital problems: 30

Any way you add the weighting factors on the above chart, the past year should have given both of us a nervous breakdown. I'm not so certain it didn't. But somehow, with the background we had, the parents who had taught us to "be tough," the belief we had in God, and the love we still had for each other, we got through all this.

One positive offshoot from the building of the largest home in Talkeetna was that word spread there was a new guy in town who knew how to build homes. This had led to a few "moonlighting" projects around town that helped our finances considerably. *Everything* wasn't turning out badly, or was it?

Talkeetna home.

"Alaskan" greenhouse —1972.

CHAPTER 15

# Mary Canary:
## *A Female Punderson*

*My father had a favorite saying:* "Never trust anyone who *insists* on doing a favor for you. The cost will be too high." Man, was he ever right.

Mary Canary was the "sweet little old lady" from whom we rented, and later bought, the old Jensen cabin in Talkeetna rather than move into the COMSAT "compound." She had insisted we rent the cabin from her at a very low monthly payment, "as a favor to her." She just *"adored"* DeAnn and all our wonderful children.

An aging widow in Texas, Mary had read an article about a famous Talkeetna bush pilot and decided to hunt him down and marry him. Hopping a ferry boat to Alaska, with her claws sharpened, she set out for the hunt. Finding the young bush pilot was not that easily ensnared, she somehow convinced the very young school principal in Talkeetna she was a qualified teacher and proceeded to earn enough money to buy the old Jensen cabin. She then engineered a fall from a ladder in the school that wrenched her back, allowing her to prematurely retire on a "disability" pension. (Several wags speculated the back injury was actually sustained from the principal bending her over his desk. But no proof was available.) Using her ill-gotten gains, she proceeded to "squat" on a prime piece of state land with a majestic view of Mt. McKinley. She began to spread the word this was her "Alaskan homestead" while conveniently ignoring the fact that this particular piece of property was not open to homesteading.

Hearing incipient complaints about Punderson and my plan to take a three-month leave of absence from COMSAT, Mary insisted on offering me a deal "too good to be true." Where was dad's advice when I really needed it?

Her deal was for me to add a wannagin to her existing house trailer already located on her "homestead." In exchange for three months' work to build her wannagin, DeAnn and I were to be given free and clear title to the Jensen cabin property. (For you cheechakos, who do not live in Alaska, a wannagin is a small framed addition attached to a house trailer, usually smaller, but never larger than the trailer.)

Carl and Lee were set to go commercial fishing with a friend of ours that summer. We shipped the three younger kids off to grandmother's in Ohio. DeAnn and I moved into a small cabin on Mary's "homestead." I proceeded to construct her little wannagin while DeAnn took up needlepoint and reading to relax. It certainly seemed to be a fun summer for us to look forward to. No Punderson to put up with.

Because the boys were not going to be available, I insisted that Mary provide a body or two to help. After disappearing to the bars in Talkeetna for a few days she reappeared dragging a hungover itinerant behind her. For room, board, and "other perks" he had agreed to be my helper. He proved to be totally useless! When he wasn't drunk, he was hungover. Over the next two months we went through several of these "helpers." All these indigents only slowed progress rather than speeding it along.

It appeared to be a slight overkill to both of us when Mary insisted the wannagin have a full foundation under it rather than the normal pilings, but since she was paying for all the materials, I never questioned it. When she asked if I could add a solid deck over the entire combination of trailer and wannagin, approximately 24' x 40', we were a bit puzzled. We reminded her I only had three months and time was growing short. She ignored us.

"DeAnn and I need to take a trip to Anchorage," Mary demanded late in June. Realizing DeAnn probably welcomed a chance to visit civilization, I did not argue.

Upon her return from Anchorage, DeAnn showed more than a little concern. "Do you realize she is planning to make a roadhouse with a bar out of this place?" she quizzed me.

"She can't do that. Alaska law requires at least ten rooms for lodging in a roadhouse with a bar," I scoffed.

"Well, she stopped and applied for a liquor license yesterday. She also stopped at United Lumber and ordered a whole bunch of materials to be delivered here."

"For what?" I scratched my head.

"I have this scary feeling we will soon find out."

Three days later a huge load of lumber was deposited in front of the trailer. "What is this for?" I asked Mary, fearing I already knew the answer.

"It is for the second floor. I need ten rooms to qualify for my liquor license. Didn't DeAnn tell you?"

"I have less than a month of my leave of absence left."

"Then finish it in the time you have left!"

"Oh come on, Mary. I thought you promised the deed to the Talkeetna lot and cabin for the wannagin. The wannagin is finished," I insisted.

"Look, you SOB, I don't give a damn what you *thought* the deal was, I get a second story or you get no deed, kapeesh?" Mary was certain she had me by the privates. So much for the "sweet old lady"!

Not being a *complete* fool, I retorted. "Okay, you win, I'll rough in your second story *after* you sign the property in Talkeetna over to us. No deed, no second story! Sign it over and I'll get as much done as I can in the next three weeks."

She was a lying crook, but not completely stupid. She knew I would uphold my side of the deal so she agreed.

"You and DeAnn go to Anchorage and find a lawyer or title company to make up the papers. De being satisfied, I will begin the top story. On your way back from town, pick up Carl and Lee. I'll need their help."

72

*I* then proceeded to get stinking drunk.

Three days later the cavalry came to my rescue. Once again, Carl and Lee, in the same spirit as the exploding stove incident, arrived with Danny Spencer, a friend of theirs. In the next three weeks, working night and day, we threw up the second story and managed to frame in and Sheetrock the small rooms and a common restroom area. You might have thought this would make Mary very grateful. But, you would have been wrong! In the middle of the night she sneaked into my temporary workshop and stole all my tools and must have sold them to some passerby. She informed us she had also filed a lien against the cabin in Talkeetna! Some nice old lady!

I wanted to kill her so bad I could taste it!

DeAnn and I packed what was left of our belongings, threw the boys in the back of our pickup, and headed to Talkeetna.

We decided to obtain a lawyer and fight the witch. We picked a lawyer from the Anchorage yellow pages and called for an appointment. DeAnn and I must have looked like two scared little kids (which we were) as we seated ourselves across the desk from this gray-haired distinguished older gentleman.

As DeAnn was slowly, and eloquently, stating our problem with Mary Canary he suddenly jumped up from his chair and shook a knurled finger in my face. "Let me tell you what happened. You somehow became acquainted with this sweet lady who talked you into a deal too good to be true. Am I right so far?" He gave us both an impish grin.

"Yes," DeAnn replied sheepishly.

"Then, after you agreed to her little suggestion, she suddenly did a metamorphosis on you and decreed that you now worked for her and whatever she said was law! Is that kind of how it went?"

"Holy cow, that's exactly what happened" DeAnn gasped, while I sat speechless and dumbfounded.

"How do you know so well what she did?" I finally managed to croak.

"I will deny having told you this, but I am her lawyer. I do not understand how two people as smart as you appear to be ever got tied up in this deal. Go home and forget about it. The problem is over."

A few weeks later we received the deed from Mary, notarized and signed over to DeAnn and me.

An honest lawyer? Of course, this was 1972 in Alaska. Most people here were still relatively honest. The two exceptions, so far, being William Punderson and Mary Canary.

As if all the other indignities forced on us by her hand were not enough, we received a $5,000 bill from United Lumber for all the materials for her second story. It seems she had convinced them she was DeAnn on one of their trips to Anchorage. I refused to pay the bill and fought United Lumber until the day they finally went out of business.

There are not many fates I can conceive of as worse than being married to Mary Canary. The young bush pilot dodged a bullet there!

CHAPTER 16

# Who the Hell Are You?

*The Mary Canary fiasco* hopefully behind us, I decided to reluctantly return to being abused by Punderson. With more than a little trepidation I approached the Talkeetna Earth Station. Much to my surprise Punderson was gone. In his place was a guy named Harry Gross. When I descended upon poor Harry to inform him that "I was back" his reply was understandably, "Who the hell are you?"

Oh-oh!

"I am Carl Gleason, the guy who took a three-month leave of absence to get his head straightened out after his dad was killed. Who are you?"

"My name is Harry Gross," he extended his hand. "Punderson told me you had resigned from COMSAT."

"Do you know Jack Williams?" I pled.

"No. Not personally."

"He is the head of personnel with COMSAT. He has my letter requesting a three-month leave. Check it out, please."

Harry's attitude did not give me a good feeling. I panicked, to say the least. Had that SOB Punderson not only won round one, but the entire match? Had the bastard managed to wipe out my leave and turn it into a resignation? I fled to Anchorage and applied for a job with ALASCOM, the newly founded long-distance carrier in Alaska. Having become well acquainted with many of the principals there, they immediately agreed to hire me as a training instructor.

Upon returning to Talkeetna, Harry met me at our home and profusely apologized for the mistake. Williams indeed verified my leave of absence. I could report for work whenever I wished.

In the space of a few hours I went from no job to a choice between two jobs. A momentous decision was called for in my relatively young life. A well-established COMSAT or the relatively new ALASCOM. Of all the bad decisions I have ever made, this was probably the most ill conceived. After conferring with my family, all of whom were in favor of remaining in Talkeetna rather than moving to Anchorage, I turned down the ALASCOM offer. After two years under COMSAT management, the Talkeetna site was sold to ALASCOM and I had a new boss. Much later, I was to learn that my new boss had taken a demotion to become the Talkeetna Earth Station manager, which my ALASCOM friends told me had been more or less promised to me (no signed contract again). Oh well, some things never change. I should have taken the original job offered by ALASCOM. This would have insured my becoming the station manager. Damn! Was anything ever going to go right in my professional life again?

**Talkeetna Bartlett Site with McKinley in the background.**

# CHAPTER 17

# Rednecks, Adventurers, Runaways, Hippies, Natives, and East Coast Jerks

## (or To Hell With All This, Let's Go Fishing!)

*Harry Gross was such* a welcome change from Punderson that we finally were able to begin to *enjoy* life in Talkeetna. DeAnn's new boss, Verne Olson, was a dedicated family man and easy man for her to work for as school secretary at the new Susitna Valley High School. I began to reflect on the past year and observe the changing scene in Talkeetna.

As I mentioned earlier, Crazy Karl, Evil Alice, and the Closes were to appear more and more "normal" as new characters surfaced in Talkeetna. I am convinced Kafka created Talkeetna. The head-on collision between the old and new cultures in 1970s Talkeetna was Kafkaesque, to say the least. The place was a microcosm of Moscow or the seedy side of New York City. The major difference being, no one in Moscow or New York knows everybody else in town. In Talkeetna, *everybody* knows *everybody* else. Isn't that a scary thought? It even grew to scare a small-town boy like me. The place holds a strange attraction for highly educated and mostly misguided souls. (Me?) If you can't make it in the real world, move to Talkeetna. Everyone there appears to share the same dreams and desires while objecting to anyone else's means of obtaining them.

A Talkeetna town meeting is like Billy Graham holding a meeting with the witches of Eastwick. How the place has not completely self-destructed over the years is a marvel. A wise woman named Nola H. Campbell wrote a wonderful book entitled *"Talkeetna Cronies"* that did a superb job of describing the values and mind-set of the few remaining adventurers in Talkeetna before the arrival of the FAA, COMSAT, and the expanded school system.

## The Adventurers:

Campbell's vivid description of the Nagleys' gallant efforts to deliver supplies to the miners in early Talkeetna and Cache Creek, Belle McDonald's adventures, and my friend Don Sheldon wonderfully captured the character of the people I came to Alaska to meet and learn from. My sons and I were very lucky to be close neighbors to Rocky Cummings, Jim Beaver, Cliff and Holly Hudson, and Don and Roberta Sheldon. Don and Cliff often gave Carl and Lee the thrill of flying to remote fishing or skiing sites. Don and Roberta, on rare occasions, graced us with their presence at parties in our home where the normally reticent Don would open up and regale everyone with stories relayed with his unique dry sense of humor. These are the adventurous people I had come to Alaska to be close with, along with the other "late" arrivals like Evil Alice, Caroll Close, and…myself.

## The Natives:

I naively thought, being a part of the Eisenhower supporters, that most of the discrimination crap was over in this wonderful country. The East Coast jerks responsible for building the Talkeetna Earth Station reminded me the battle had still not been won. Several local natives, of the Athabascan Indian descent, were hired as "grunt" labor to help construct the site.

Being typically East Coast, the contractors daily left the site to eat lunch at Fairview, Teepee, or Roadhouse in downtown Talkeetna. The natives would be left there to eat their packed lunches of jerky, smoked salmon, or moose sandwiches while talking about tomorrow's big fishing trip or moose hunt. By no accident I began to carry my own lunch and stay behind to eavesdrop on these enticing discourses. What a wonderful experience this was to become. I soon learned they enjoyed (excuse me, my "native" friends) listening to the condescending East Coast snobs talk down to them about how they were going to get the government to help them solve their "problems." In my mind, and theirs, there just ain't any problem!

One result of these new friendships was that I was invited to go on fishing trips to "secret" holes filled with trout, dolly varden, grayling, and salmon. Upon returning from an always successful fishing trip my standard instruction was always the same: "If anybody asks you where you caught these fish, tell them behind the Rainbow Lodge." The slough behind the lodge was always packed with cheechakos (greenhorn) fishermen wondering why the fish had quit biting. For added excitement, the slough was also a favorite hangout for many of the local *bears!*

If you want to know the real meaning of life in Alaska, talk to my old fishing and drinking buddies, the Nikolai brothers, or others like them.

## *The Hippies and Runaways Versus the Rednecks:*

It seems being overrun by the FAA, COMSAT, and the flood of new school employees wasn't punishment enough for the Talkeetna natives and old "redneck" adventurers who originally settled the area. In the early 1970s the State of Alaska decided to open the area just north of town to five-acre "homesites." This was an open invitation for every derelict, doper, dropout, and California "wannabe hippie" type to squat and hide away in their own little Alaskan hovel while continuing to collect their welfare checks from Uncle Sam.

What everyone forgot to tell these idiots was that it gets *very cold* in the part of the country where they were throwing up their uninsulated tents and stick huts. The first cold snap of the year produced a never-ending stream of raggedly clad urchins falling off the train from the north and straggling into the nearest warm haven with frostbitten toes, fingers, and cheeks. What a pitiful sight!

The nearest warm spot to the train depot was the Fairview Inn, hangout for most of the old "redneck" cronies in town. Tiring of being invaded by these half-frozen "hippies," the Fairview owner hung a sign on the front door reading: "Hippies use side door." The side door held a similar sign reading: "Closed." Tensions mounted. Before the long winter ended, most everyone in town was housing an unwelcome guest or two. What else were they to do with them?

Evil Alice, the Closes, and most other merchants around town manufactured a few odd jobs to help keep them in pocket money when their welfare ran out, none of which was fully appreciated.

# CHAPTER 18

# My John Wayne Period

*The primary reason for* building the Talkeetna satellite communications site was to provide economical communications to the Lower 48 during construction of the oil pipeline from Prudhoe Bay to Valdez.

There is no way an impulsive and reckless-abandon type could have been in Alaska at this time and not have become involved with the pipeline.

When ALASCOM bought the Talkeetna site from COMSAT, all COMSAT personnel were given the choice of staying in Alaska with ALASCOM or moving on to other COMSAT locations in the Lower 48. For some strange reason I decided to stay in Talkeetna, at DeAnn's urging.

ALASCOM was internally advertising for a "John Wayne" type communications manager on the Arctic North Slope. What the hell, who was more John Wayne than me? I was 6'2' and 200 pounds. I was raised on a farm where my brothers and I broke horses for my dad. I was raised to be tough.

I applied for the job more to get away from the day-to-day tedium of family life with a wife who had grown rather distant to me. I got the job, which required my spending about 80 percent of my time away from home. If I couldn't get her to leave the state, I would get even by taking a job that got me as far away from the house as possible. What a coward! Some John Wayne I was.

My arrival at Camp Galbraith, my new headquarters as North Slope Manager for ALASCOM, promptly dispelled any myth of being "John Wayne." I was greeted by an extremely disgruntled group of technicians who were not bashful about letting me know they expected only support and no bullshit from a new manager. Except for one, an always smiling guy named Larry Clasen, all of the technicians were older than me and obviously viewed me as a new kid on the block who could be bossed by *them.*

My old AT&T experience promptly came into play. Hopefully, I could avoid some of the mistakes I, as a kid supervisor, had made back then. "Have at it, men. I've been here before. Shoot!" I insisted.

"No one respects us," Assbo shouted.

"Hire more natives!" Haldane screamed.

"F' you!" Assbo used his favorite expletive and finger to Haldane.

"Tough crowd," I was thinking to myself. "What have I started here?"

I looked at Clasen. He gave no indication of support or non-support. My God, what happened to John Wayne? Mommy! "Okay, what in the hell is your biggest problem? I'll deal with it first."

A long silence set in. Finally Clasen drawled, "Guess they just want to know if you are for real or just another bullshitter."

"Hell, guys, the only way you will ever know if I'm for real is if you come to me with your problems and I solve them, I guess. I will tell you this. I will not ever lie to you and I expect the same from each of you. Fair enough?"

Another hour of petty bickering. Where the hell *is* John Wayne when you need him? Several grueling hours later, everybody seemed to finally be talked out and the meeting dissolved. I slunk off to find my new bed.

On Alaska's North Slope the weather was a vicious adversary. If it wasn't the cold, it was the wind. Mostly it was the cold *and* the wind.

We were isolated in our own small group with no way in or out except by air taxi services, whose schedule was controlled by the weather. Anyone who claimed he could spend more than the normal six-week tour in the isolation, more often than not went a little crazy and began to break up everything in sight. In my camp, and every other camp north of the Yukon River, all of the problems eventually came to me. Everyone attempted to control their emotions by...gambling...booze...or both. I chose booze. Gambling might have been a better choice. Who knows?

Daily, someone was stranded on a mountaintop site by weather, or an expensive piece of equipment would be dropped over a cliff, having slipped the grasp of a helicopter. Power generator failures or fuel shortages at remote sites while a technician or mechanic was stranded there in subzero weather was always a dangerous possibility. I instituted a policy whereby it was left to the discretion of the helicopter pilots as to whether or not we flew people in on any given day. This didn't make my boss very happy, but it sure pleased my people.

Our maintenance section of the pipeline stretched from Prudhoe Bay to just north of the Yukon River, nearly half of the 800-mile pipeline. Rather than follow the original plan of having every technician's bed at Galbraith, and travel daily up to and over a hundred miles to one of the other camps or pump stations, I visited with each of the Alyeska Camp managers and asked to have a bed at each camp for an in-house technician. The camp managers loved the idea and so did the technicians. I then began to personally train Clasen in every phase of the network so as to make him a "floating" technician who would fill in for technicians who were on their two-week leave after spending six weeks at their site. I kept Haldane, the least experienced, at Galbraith as my personal aid, allowing me to train him also. He really appreciated that.

Gradually, the petty bickering faded away and the crew became as happy as possible under near impossible odds.

I began to dread taking my own leave time as, upon my return, my meddling boss had always managed to tick everybody off by rearranging their schedules or some other unnecessary change in prearranged plans. Also, my week at home was invariably too short to accomplish DeAnn's "Honey-do" list. Frustrating.

After about a year and a half, the climax of my North Slope career and my communications career, for the second time in my life, came over a matter of right versus wrong. Sometimes you must take a stand. One of my employees was stealing equipment and warehousing it for sale in Fairbanks. Due to rather lax security, too much of this sort of thing was occurring during the pipeline construction. I could have looked the other way. I could have done like some of the other managers and asked for a cut of the take. I chose the moral route, firing the labor union employee. Although my immediate superior gave lip service in my support, from that day forward most major decisions went around me between my boss and the local union steward, Assbo. I accidently learned of this little bit of deception by monitoring a telephone conversation between them.

Sometimes a sense of morality can be a dangerous thing for a career.

I have no strong feeling one way or the other toward labor unions. Over the years I have belonged to several unions. I have managed union organized and unorganized people. Good workers are good workers, as a matter of conscience. Deadbeats and troublemakers exist in both groups.

I would like to say I graciously resigned my command. But instead, I jumped in my private airplane and had the pilot fly me to Fairbanks. Storming into the vice president's office, my boss, I threw my company keys in the middle of his desk, issued a string of ill-chosen expletives and slammed the door behind me as I exited. If you are going to be John Wayne, be John Wayne all the way. At least I didn't hit him.

End of North Slope and communications career.

Who cared?

CHAPTER 19

# New Career; New Life

It *was 1977 and we* were both now forty years old. To date, we had been sticking it out in Alaska for seven years. We now had two college-bound sons and three teenagers still at home. And I was once again unemployed.

After twenty-two years of marriage, DeAnn had come to realize that while employed, I was an excellent provider, but I had this tendency to develop this recurring "midlife crisis" type syndrome every ten years or so. While I was playing around on the North Slope, DeAnn had rekindled her own career, partly to help smooth over the rough spots created by my reckless and impulsive foot-shooting stages and partly to get the younger kids and herself *out* of Talkeetna.

Finally! She had done on her own what I had been attempting to push her to do for over six years. She was leaving Talkeetna. Thank God!

The real estate career she had attempted to start while I was still employed by AT&T back in Ohio had been abruptly terminated when I jerked her to West Virginia and Talkeetna. Having slightly freed herself from me while I was playing John Wayne, she used this golden opportunity to earnestly pursue a real estate career in Alaska.

My short tenure on the Slope had provided one big advantage—a huge paycheck. This had resulted in a large savings account.

DeAnn had wisely used some of this income to establish her career as a real estate broker. After consulting with me, she listed our home in Talkeetna for sale and began to prepare to move our family to Wasilla, the fastest growing area in Alaska. We decided to use most of our bankroll to build our dream home in Wasilla.

Over the years, we had designed and redesigned this home several times. A lot with a great view of the mountains was a must, in our minds. We found the perfect lot. Carl, Lee, my brother James (who had returned to Alaska) and I built a beautiful three-story, 3,500-square-foot home. The home was shaped like a pentagon. It had an open circular stairway that wound up the center of the house from first to third level. The lower level was a huge recreation room with a marble fireplace, laundry, and full bath with a Jacuzzi and sauna. The main floor had a 20' x 50' cathedral living-and-dining room with another huge marble fireplace, kitchen, master bedroom, and bath. The top floor contained two more large bedrooms and another full bath. The front, and both sides of the house had large decks facing the beautiful Talkeetna and Chugach Mountains.

We lived in the home for only one year. DeAnn had a customer stop into her office, who wanted to buy the "nicest home for sale in the valley." They could afford to pay in excess of $100,000. DeAnn informed them there were no homes for sale in that category. At the time, the average price for homes in the Wasilla area was about $50,000.

"Would you like to contact a builder and see if one would be willing to take your design and build a new home for you?"

"No. My husband is the new manager for this borough, we have a family to get into school and do not want the hassle of building," the wife answered.

"Isn't there a home, which if it were for sale, would be in the $100,000 price range that you know of? Maybe we could at least look at one to give us an idea what we could buy for that amount," the new borough manager asked.

"Well…there is one that I know of, but it isn't for sale."

"Can we at least *look* at it?" they begged.

"Okay, follow me in your car. It's about two miles from here." DeAnn guided them to our new home. She opened the main door.

The wife immediately exclaimed, "I must have this house! Tell the owner to name the price. We'll pay it!"

"The price would depend on what the bank would appraise it for," DeAnn informed her.

"What would you estimate the appraisal to be?"

"Probably in the range of $100,000," DeAnn sighed.

"We'll pay whatever it appraises for. Can we talk to the owner?" the manager demanded.

"You are...." DeAnn had to sit down. Her knees were too shaky to stand.

"Is it a deal?" the woman pled.

"If my husband agrees...I suppose so." Good-bye dream home.

The combined effort between my sons, my brother, and me was so successful we decided to take some of the profit from our dream home and follow my father's footsteps into homebuilding. With DeAnn being a broker, it became a natural and very profitable arrangement.

Neither Carl nor Lee had been that wild about college life anyway.

We devoted the following six to seven years to growing and expanding our businesses. DeAnn became a partner in one of the largest real estate firms in the area. My little company expanded to three companies. While continuing the original construction company, we started the first private fee home inspection company in Alaska. I also started a small communications consulting company. Communications was creeping back into my life.

With acquisition of wealth also seems to come the need to increase your social and political exposure. During this time we both became very active socially and politically. De was elected president of the Matauska-Susitna Valley Board of Realtors. She also held various positions on the state Board of Realtors for more than ten years. She was Alaska Realtor of the Year for 1981. We had developed a very close working relationship, which set us back on the road to a completely restored loving and caring personal relationship.

This stage in our lives was, I believe, a maturing period for me. I even ran for political office as a member of the Wasilla city council. I lost, in a very close race. This ended my political ambitions.

At last success had found us.

CHAPTER 20

# Questover:
## *DeAnn Chimes in Again*

*Other than dragging us* all to Alaska, in my opinion at the time, the dumbest thing C. David (by this time he had completely dropped the Carl and was going by C. David) ever did was buy Questover.

In 1981, I listed a forty-acre piece of property on Fish Creek, seventeen miles from downtown Wasilla, where my real estate office was at the time. I informed every agent in my office that they were *NOT* to tell my husband of this listing.

Fortunately, I managed to sell Questover before C. David knew anything about this 3,500-square-foot combination of four connected dome buildings on a forty-acre piece of property located on the best salmon fishing stream in the area.

But…the new buyer had found a moisture problem with one of the domes housing the master bedroom and bath. He contacted me and I asked the sellers, Ray and Thelma Gudreau, to meet me at Questover, hoping to solve the problem.

Ray asked me to have a building contractor meet us at the home. Knowing the home was already sold, I asked C. David to go with me as owner of Gleason Builders, one of his companies at the time. After all, the place was already sold, right?

As C. David and I drove down the mile-long driveway to Questover he casually asked, "You had this property listed and never told me?"

"Uh, yea. But it is already sold," I weakly replied.

We arrived at the huge dome. C. David dove from the car and began to survey the area. "That is Fish Creek," he almost screamed as he looked at the beautiful stream below the dome.

Ray Gudreau and *another* Karl, the very unhappy buyer, met us near a hole in the ground that Karl had dug to reveal a few rotten floor joists at one end of the four dome structures comprising Questover.

"This place hates us," Karl was screaming. "Water is flooding into this area. The main dome is also flooding. The stove quit working. You have sold us a rotten pumpkin!"

Very calmly, Ray replied with "What do you want me to do to fix this problem?"

"Tear down and replace this part of the rotten pumpkin."

Ray turned to C. David and asked, "How much to replace it?"

"Twenty-five thousand," he guessed.

"Okay," he wrote out a check for twenty-five thousand. "If you need any more, let me know." *Wow!*

It was October, in Alaska. By the time our sons and C. David tore down the old dome, not an easy project, and built a replacement, it was November. Domes do *not* just fall down.

They placed several electric heaters under the new structure to dry out the crawl space and new construction. They cautioned Karl to leave them on.

After his first electric bill, Karl decided to shut off the electric heaters. If fate had not been so unkind he might have gotten away with turning off the heaters. However, it was thirty degrees below zero when he turned off the heat. The entire damp structure turned to ice. The following week the temperatures rose to forty degrees *above* zero. All of the ice in the new structure began to melt! Not only the new structure, but most of the original dome began to rain on the inhabitants. Karl panicked. He called me, and I called Ray and Thelma Gudreau. Ray and Thelma flew from Hawaii to Alaska in hopes of solving this problem.

Thelma and C. David (who she ever after called her grandson) formed an immediate bond. She recognized the "old farm boy" in him and played it like a virtuoso. Ray immediately picked up on this and presented Karl with a deal too good to refuse.

"What will it take to make you happy?" Ray asked Karl.

"This place hates us. I want out of it," Karl responded.

"You have twenty-five thousand invested here. Suppose I give you a thirty-thousand-dollar, five-acre plot on the other end of the homestead?"

"Sounds good to me," Karl jumped.

"DeAnn, sell this 'rotten pumpkin' to somebody else, but don't give them the same reverse amortization deal we gave Karl."

"Really," C. David responded. "I was about to offer you the same deal!"

"Sold!" Ray and Thelma chorused. Over my objections, C. David purchased Questover.

Okay, fine. We have spent twenty-four of the most enjoyable years of our lives at Questover. Most of our children have chosen to be married at Questover. All of our grandchildren have learned how to work, fish, and garden here. C. David subdivided eleven acres of Questover and made it into our retirement. The fish, garden, and winery at Questover have made us more healthy and happy than most.

What more do you want me to say? *He was right, okay?!*

But, the most wonderful offshoot of Questover has been the "Camp Questover" started by me in 1993. Only grandkids were invited. No parents! C. David and I gave certificates for:

- Most fish
- Biggest fish
- Best croquet player
- Best softball team and player
- Best volleyball team
- Winners of scavenger hunt as a team
- Most helpful to Grandma
- Most congenial
- Best sport

This system has gone on for over ten years. The older group are now all teenagers. Yet, they still ask us every year, "When is next year's Camp Questover?" Okay, C. David, for the last time, you were right to buy Questover. Enough said.

# Camp Questover

Questover—today.

First "Big Kids" camp, 1992.

Camp Questover, 1996.

Camp Questover, 2000.

Last "Big Kids" camp, 2003.

"Little Kids" Camp Questover, 2003.

# CHAPTER 21

# The Alaskan Crash of 1985 from C. David's Point of View

*The price of oil,* due to whatever was behind the scenes, dropped from over twenty dollars per barrel to less than seven dollars. To the Alaskan economy this was a death blow. To us it was a personal financial death blow.

The crash happened so quickly most Alaskans had no time to prepare.

Our construction company was in the process of building several single- and multifamily homes. All of the prospective buyers lost their jobs due to the oil company slowdowns. The homes became *ours,* at a high rate of interest payments on interim loans.

Real estate sales stopped.

Our office rental space became vacant.

We had several thousand dollars in cash reserves. We rapidly depleted this in an attempt to stay solvent.

*Bankrupt,* financially and morally.

If you have a conscience, when you fall into this situation, you begin to dwell on all of the lives you have so adversely affected. Thinking about all the jobs you have eliminated and all the turmoil you have caused in the lives of people you can no longer provide salaries, hospitalization, and security for can drive you crazy. I did dwell on this, a lot! It did drive me crazy, a lot! I began to drink again, a lot!

There is something very different about tragedy caused by your own impulsive and reckless behavior versus tragedy caused by someone else's impulsive and reckless behavior. In the past, when the situation was brought about by my own actions, I still felt a sense of control. In this circumstance I felt like a helpless, abused, and injured child.

As a result of the crash:

- My brother left the state of Alaska, again.
- Carl joined the navy.
- Lee became a truck driver.
- Our youngest, Patrick, became confused. (Join the crowd!)
- DeAnn merged her real estate company with a larger corporation in Anchorage.

All we had left was each other. In retrospect, that was more than most people had.

Remember, when God closes a door he always leaves a window open....

# CHAPTER 22

# Our Peak Career Years of Being *In Demand*

## *(or Never Make an Enemy You Don't Need)*

*At age forty-eight,* both of our careers took a sharp turn. From this point on neither of us again *applied* for a job. All potential employers came to us.

One of my communications consulting contracts had been for a small company, GCI, that was hoping to compete with my old employer, ALASCOM. They initially contacted me to help engineer and monitor the building, testing, and turn-up of their first satellite earth stations in Alaska and Washington State. They were also looking for an operations supervisor to hire, train, and supervise the new technical force they hoped to assemble. The word of my "key tossing" resignation from ALASCOM had preceded me. They offered me the job.

How could an impulsive and reckless guy turn *this* opportunity down? Not to mention a guy who was broke and had no other apparent options.

Over the next four years, GCI expanded to the point where we had nearly half the long distance business in Alaska. This became a period of rejuvenation for me. I regained some of the old competitive spirit that had been buried in the crash of 1985.

On the negative side, I did redevelop some of the old management style that had caused me so many problems with my first AT&T management position. My force-fed training and management style worked fine while GCI was a highly competitive underdog company. However, in today's world of what some call "love-in management" versus success at any price, my style began to outlive its usefulness. The vice president I reported to repeatedly asked me to back off from my "micromanagement" techniques. I did...for me.

While attempting to readjust my style I was also attempting to, unsuccessfully, interest GCI in the latest satellite technology. My boss was convinced it would never work in Alaska. I used his lack of foresight as my excuse to resign. At least I left on relatively good terms this time. A first for me.

Two friends of mine had already left GCI to implement a satellite earth station utilizing the new Ku Band technology I had been trying to force GCI into. They asked me to join their new company, PDI, as their engineering manager. *Finally,* back to the profession I loved most! This all proved that at age fifty I could still be impulsive and reckless. The main differences being that I had burned no bridges as I shot myself in the foot. Or so I thought...

When you set out to compete with a company still hungering to devour all its competitors, be very careful.

By everyone's working night and day, our new Ku Band company was managing to become a financial success. We were expanding the latest direct digital private line services throughout the city of Anchorage. In addition, we were using the new, and more economical, Ku Band satellite technology to provide switched voice services to the rest of the world, thus competing directly with GCI and ALASCOM.

In a small struggling company such as PDI, the engineering manager wears many hats. One of my many hats was to serve as technical support for our sales people making pitches to potential customers. One of those potential customers was the FAA. We paid several visits to their representatives, in attempts to explain the new technology. Fortunately, many of these federal people remembered me.

Finally tiring of our stealing customers from them, GCI approached the stockholders st PDI while I was on a trip to Washington State. Upon my return, I learned that I now, once again, worked for GCI. Until my first paycheck came along with more than a thousand-dollars-per-month decrease in my salary, this didn't appear to be that bad of a turn.

I got the message.

Meanwhile, one of the FAA people contacted me and asked if I'd be interested in hiring on with a consulting firm to help them design a Ku Band system for Alaska. "Why not?"

During this hectic period in my life, DeAnn was once again revitalizing her real estate career. This time it was in Anchorage. Her past service as Valley Board president, State President Elect, and Alaska Realtor of the Year made her a well-known name in the Alaska real estate community. Several offices in Anchorage were openly courting her to join their firms.

Unwisely, she chose to accept an offer from a well known "good Christian" Anchorage businessman. He convinced her to become the broker in a new firm bearing his name. He promised to throw money at her to spend however she wished in establishing the office. She was to have a free hand and not expected to produce any real profit for at least three years.

She would receive only a nominal salary and be a "working" broker to supplement her income with commissions during the building phase.

This all seemed to be reasonable thinking (at the time).

# CHAPTER 23

# My Long Year as a Government Consultant

## *(or Why Your Taxes Are So High)*

*Politically, I may be* just a little to the right of Rush Limbaugh, which is quite possibly why I lost the only political race I ever entered. Today, in Alaska, I could probably win.

With my political slant in mind, it is hard to imagine I could become a government consultant. I did.

As previously suggested, Alaska is a natural environment for satellite communications. Most of the state has no connecting roads. Some fifty to sixty villages are accessible only by air. To put this in perspective, if you place a map of Alaska over the top of a map of the contiguous forty-eight states:

Point Barrow Alaska is located over Duluth, Minnesota.

Anchorage is located over Oklahoma City.

Adak is located over San Diego.

Ketchican falls over South Carolina.

*All* of the connecting roads in Alaska would be contained inside Oklahoma, Kansas and Missouri. The picture being that Alaska is a vast area roughly one-fifth the size of the Lower 48, lightly populated, with most areas connected by airplanes. No roads.

The FAA approached me with the above mentioned map. They hired me to design an *economical* satellite system to provide emergency backup communications between the fifteen major radar, air-to-ground control sites in Alaska and the Air Traffic Control Center in Anchorage.

The original Ku Band system, as suggested by the FAA project manager and designed by me, was a good one.

They asked me to accompany them to Washington, DC, and present our plan to the budget committees in the House and Senate. Getting to hobnob with senators and congressmen was pretty heady stuff for this old farm boy. We were also wined and dined by the heads of many Fortune 500 companies who would be competing for the contract to build this embryonic system.

A few times during these trips to DC, it did cross my mind that an awful lot of attention was being given to my little $15 million dollar project. However, when you were raised on Walton Mountain, as I was, you still hang on to not always suspecting the worst in people.

Returning from the third trip to DC, the FAA project manager approached me. A large government contractor had been hired to build my system. He had convinced them to hire me, at a fabulous salary, to stay on as the technical consultant.

In my opinion, through deception, half truths, sleight of hand, innuendo, and outright bald-faced lies, the large contractor who purchased my little $15 million dollar project, managed to turn it into a $200 million dollar boondoggle.

I protested.

I fussed.

I fumed.

I talked to my congressman, for whom I had campaigned hard to help elect.

I considered complaining to both of our senators, whom DeAnn and I knew personally. But…I had helped convince them this project was a good idea. Catch-22.

Everybody else associated with the project quit talking to me. For nearly a year I sat all alone and undisturbed in a huge office, collecting my grand salary. *Boring and criminal.*

# CHAPTER 24

# 1989: The Last Big Career Move for Me
## *(I Think!)*

*While struggling to* endure the humiliation of being an unused government consultant, some of the dispossessed people from PDI were toying with the idea of doing business in Russia.

These young entrepreneurs were in search of a "mature" project and engineering manager to interface with the Russians, whom it appeared did not give much credibility to these young Americans.

So it had finally come to this. I was to become an "elder statesman."

These were the very early years of Glasnost and Perestroika (roughly translated as the opening up of Russian society to Western culture, and political and economic discussions in hopes of stealing our technology). The plan was that my potential new boss and I would fly from Anchorage through Paris to Moscow in November. After meeting with the Moscow people who were to finance the proposed project, we would fly via the Russian airline, Aeroflot, on to Irkutsk on Lake Baikal in central Siberia. After meeting with the potential Russian customers in Irkutsk, we would take Aeroflot on to Khabarovsk, on the Chinese border just North of Vladivostok. After meeting with the Khabarovsk customers, we would fly North to Magadhan and on home to Anchorage.

I thought, "What the heck? The free trip around the world alone is worth the time and effort. Why not?"

I applied for vacation time, deciding to remain in my "non job" consulting position while enjoying this new adventure. Because I had no real duties, I occupied my time listening to Russian language tapes. DeAnn and I decided to take Russian language classes evenings at Alaska University. We practiced speaking Russian with each other. I also brushed up on my French, as my new boss and I were scheduled to spend an eight-hour layover in Paris with time to do a little sightseeing.

DeAnn was now literally working day and night to get her new company off the ground. I was stagnating professionally and eagerly looking for a new challenge.

It is a little hard to admit that I was feeling so elated at the prospect of traveling around the world as an "elder statesman" for a company. It was the opportunity of a lifetime for this little old farm boy.

I had finally reached my ultimate potential.

If you are interested in learning of how my "ultimate potential" was put to use please purchase and read my book, *Why Russia? A Nostalgic Old World Adventure,* from Fish Creek Publishing, P.O. Box 871007, Wasilla, Alaska 99687.

# EPILOGUE

*We still have a* few old friends living in Talkeetna. Every time we travel the Parks Highway our thoughts drift back to that small part of our lives. Our Talkeetna life now seems almost a dream or a story of another young couple's life, relayed to us over some late night campfire by our favorite fishing stream. Or perhaps it never really happened at all....It was only a dream.

Traveling north of Talkeetna, thoughts drift back to precious times spent picking blueberries around Byers Lake with our children, trudging to the mouth of Troublesome Creek to catch too many kings to carry, or the spot where Hans and I bagged our last moose together.

The old lodge with the house trailer hidden underneath is still standing. As we pass, we feel a twinge of remorse over the heartaches involved with another dream gone astray and a friendship lost forever.

Life on the last frontier has been filled with many good times. It has also brought some bad times that cause us to wonder from time to time how different things might have been had we never made this bold step. That is something we will never know.

**Mount McKinley.**

# Give the Gift of
# Why Alaska?
## Life on the Last Frontier
## to Your Friends and Colleagues

CHECK YOUR LEADING BOOKSTORE,
AMAZON.COM OR ORDER HERE

❏ **YES**, I want _____ copies of *Why Alaska? Life on the Last Frontier* at $9.95 each, plus $4.95 shipping per book.

❏ **YES**, I want _____ copies of *Why Russia? A Nostalgic Old World Adventure* at $14.95 each, plus $4.95 shipping per book.

*Canadian orders must be accompanied by a postal money order in U.S. funds. Allow 15 days for delivery.*

My check or money order for $_____ is enclosed.

Name _____

Organization _____

Address _____

City/State/Zip _____

Phone_____ E-mail _____

*Please make your check payable and return to:*

### Fish Creek Publishing
P.O. Box 871007
Wasilla, Alaska 99687

# Why Russia?

If you've enjoyed *Why Alaska? Life on the Last Frontier,*
you'll also want to read

## Why Russia? A Nostalgic Old World Adventure

(228 pages, illustrated, indexed, copyright 2002).

The events in *Why Russia?* pick up where *Why Alaska?* leaves off. It is an autobiographical account of C. David Gleason's business experiences in Russia and his encounter with what Winston Churchill called "a riddle wrapped in a mystery inside an enigma." This memoir chronicles the author's professional dealings as a communications engineer and consultant, and his indelible experiences with the Russian people.

*Why Russia?: A Nostalgic Old World Adventure* may be purchased for $14.95 plus $4.95 shipping from Fish Creek Publishing, P.O. Box 871007, Wasilla, Alaska 99687. (See order form on reverse. Canadian orders must be accompanied by a postal money order in U.S. funds. Allow 15 days for delivery.) It is also available through Amazon.com.